The Killing Pens

The Killing Pens

Janet Hughes

Laurels Publications

First published in 2004 by:
Laurels Publications,
Churchstoke,
Powys, SY15 6SR.

Tel: 01588 620591
e-mail: laurels.j@tiscali.co.uk

ISBN: 0-9548620-0-7

British Library Cataloguing in Publication Data
A catalogue record for this book is available from the British Library.

Proceeds from the sale of this book will be used for a memorial fund for the animals. Further copies may be purchased from: Janet Hughes, Laurels Publications, Laurels Cottage, Churchstoke, Montgomery, Powys, SY15 6SR. Please send a cheque payable to Save Our Sheep Fund for £12 plus £2 p&p per copy for UK mainland delivery; £4 for overseas delivery.

Printed by Welshpool Printing Group

FOR FREDDY

Little Lamb who made thee
Dost thou know who made thee
Gave thee life and bid thee feed.
By the stream and oe'r the mead;
Gave thee clothing of delight,
Softest clothing woolly bright;
Gave thee such a tender voice,
Making all the vales rejoice!

Songs of Innocence (1789) 'The Lamb'
William Blake 1757-1827

Contents

Acknowledgements 11

Foreword by Christopher Booker 13

Introduction by Sue Burton, Remus Memorial Horse Sanctuary, Essex 17

PART ONE – ROAD TO THE CASE

1 A Journey 21
2 The Court 23
3 Outbreak 26
4 Meetings 31
5 Warning 36
6 Trip to London 38
7 Meeting Theo 41
8 Chilled Milk 44
9 The Crying Lady 48
10 Hannah 54
11 Rainbows and Flames 57
12 Four Crosses 60
13 Easter 63
14 The Gelli Sheep 66
15 Mrs Jones 70
16 The FMD Truth Rally 73
17 Election Day Dragon 77
18 Fears of Mass Cull 82
19 One for Sorrow 85
20 Libanus 87
21 Wolverhampton 89
22 The Lion Hotel and More Meetings 91
23 The Pens 95
24 Black Friday 99

PART TWO – THE CASE

25	Birthday Gifts	102
26	Making a Start	107
27	Ten Sheep	111
28	Donors and Drunks	115
29	The Judge's Decision	122
30	Morning in Court	126
31	Luncheon Panic	133
32	The Afternoon Judgment	135
33	Journey Home	142
34	Media Post-Mortem	144
35	Preparations for Appeal	147
36	'Angels of Death'	150
37	Bristol Meetings	155
38	Mrs Powell and her Rams	162
39	Message on a Train	165
40	Meeting at Merthyr Tydfil	171
41	Deception	174
42	Christmas Preparations	177
43	Bird Song	181
44	Fire Drill	184
45	Endings and Beginnings	190
46	Resource Planning Team	194
47	The Last Resort	201

PART THREE – THE AFTERMATH

48	The Two Crows	205
49	The Elusive Writ	209
50	The Umbrella Man	212
51	Discoveries	215
52	Pound of Flesh	220
53	Letting Go	225
	Epilogue	231

APPENDICES

1	Test results for Brecon Beacons Hefts	235
2	List of test results for Infected Premises in Wales	236

Certain individuals remain anonymous for legal reasons.

Acknowledgements

Special thanks to my son Matthew and my partner Glyn, for their unfailing support throughout.

I wish to express my gratitude to all the following people, who helped in many different ways:

The many generous, kind people who gave donations to the 'Save Our Sheep Fund' and for helping us when we were in trouble in 2003;

Phoebe and Dennis Hughes, our dear friends, who tried so hard to save their flock of sheep;

The late Professor Fred Brown, for his expert advice during the case;

Christopher Booker, for writing the foreword and for reporting on the case in 2003;

Sue Burton, for her friendship, help and faith in the case and for writing the introduction; Mavis Petrie, for her help and kindness; Pat Innocent, for being there all along the way in the courts; Mary Critchley, for her help and invaluable information; Christine Ball for her optimism and friendship; Kate Gorman; Tracey Jones; Alistair McConnachie; Astrid Goddard; Jane Barribal; Jan Edwards; Dafydd Morris; David Gatehouse; Marlene Morgan; Eirwen Harry; Nicola Morris; Eurig Wyn MEP; David Lidington MP; Carly Thrale; Stephen Tromans; David Greenhalgh; Jason McCue; Zac Goldsmith; Joanna Cash; Professors David Campbell and

Robert Lee; Tim Rhys; Dr Richard North; Rob Shelley, Abigail Hart, and Frank Lockyer of ITV Wales; Penny Roberts of BBC Wales; Karen Evans; Christy Tuer; Anwen Evans; Sue Goddard; David Adams; Leslie Blohm; Guy Adams; Adrian Foulkes of Flanagan and Jones; Laura Wurzal; Bryn Thomas and particularly Mr John Wilkins, for dreaming of sheep.

Stephen Williams, farmer in the Brecon Beacons National Park, for 'selling' me 10 sheep, which made the case possible.

The slaughter man, for his honesty and for his help in preventing further mass culls.

Marjorie Jones, and Maureen Williams, local farmers, for their kind support.

Al Jones and Richard Stanton, for their kind permission to use their photographs.

Ray Edgar, for use of his photograph of the Welsh Mountain Sheep.

I also wish to thank the following people for making the publication of this book possible: Sue Burton; David Harcombe; Godfrey Nall; Michael Smith; Mr Horne; Mrs Stark; Daniel Margolis; Jill Evans; Mr Ainsworth; Colonel and Mrs Turner; Colin Strang Steel; Madge Allen; Chris Phillips; Christine Ball; Myra, USA; Betty, New Zealand; Juanita Wilson, Mossburn Animal Sanctuary; Professor Sheila Crispin; Elise Lambert-Gorwyn; Anne Dick; Roger Ledger; Anne Lambourn; Jackie Short; Delaine Haynes; Dr Theresa Watts; Stella Masters; Frank Hughes; Pat Innocent; Jane Barribal; Jill Britten; Margaret Metcalf; Hilary Peters; Jillian Atkins; Alison Crisp; Fiona Palmer; Mona Parr; Mary Critchley; Anthony Reed; Jill Byron; Joan Cambage; Roger Windsor; Victoria Mills; Carol Kay; Eirwen Harry; Pat Walker

Finally, last but certainly not least, all of our lovely cats and dogs who comforted me along the way: Sally, Bess, Holly, Bobby, Daisy, Henry, Rolo, Billy, Tilly, Poppy, Lottie and Solomon.

Foreword

In more than 40 years as a journalist, I have never covered a story remotely like that of the 2001 foot and mouth disaster. During that year, in the Sunday Telegraph, the Daily Mail and Private Eye, I wrote more words about that dreadful crisis than anyone.

There were two features of this story which made it an unprecedented chapter in our national life. The first was the grotesque incompetence with which the Blair government responded to the epidemic, killing millions of healthy animals in an orgy of slaughter which was not justified either by science or the law. This amounted, as I wrote at the time, to one of the greatest acts of maladministration by any British government in history.

The other was the horrendous damage and pain the government's actions inflicted on Britain's rural communities, and on all those directly involved – countless thousands of farmers and their families, and those who struggled against all odds to keep afloat every kind of rural business. For many of them those months were like living through some unreal nightmare, a cross between Kafka and Dostoevsky.

If ever a real-life drama deserved to be recorded in a book it was this one, and there are two general ways in which this might be done. One is to try to give an overview of the whole story, from the conduct of the politicians and their advisers 'at the top', right down to the consequences of their decisions as these affected 'ordinary people', in Cumbria, Devon and north Yorkshire, in the west Midlands and in Wales. That is what Dr Richard North and I tried to do in our account of the story, Not The Foot And Mouth Report, published by Private Eye in September 2001.

The other approach is to give a detailed eyewitness account of the crisis by someone who was directly involved. And in that respect no one is better qualified by the remarkable part she played in the story at the time than the author of this book, Janet Hughes.

Those awful, confused, tragic months threw up a good many heroic individuals: people who bravely tried to stand up for truth and decency when the politicians and their officials, like an army of Orcs, were trampling both into the bloodstained earth.

One such was Professor Fred Brown, the lovable Lancastrian who was perhaps the world's leading veterinary expert on FMD and who, right from the start, with his admirable Dutch colleague Dr Simon Barteling was pleading for the government to use vaccination, to stop the insane slaughter. Another was Mary Critchley, an English teacher living in France, who from her home near Bordeaux managed to create an incredibly professional website, which more than anything else helped to keep those centrally involved in the battle informed as to what was going on.

But the heroine whose experience did perhaps more than anyone's to bring home the Kafkaesque nature of this story was Janet Hughes. The glory of what she did was that, as an environmental science teacher living in mid-Wales, she watched the crisis unfolding around her until eventually she decided to intervene herself – in a truly extraordinary and courageous way.

The greatest single blunder of the government's response to the epidemic was to order the slaughter of some nine million healthy animals: the so-called 'pre-emptive cull'. The point, as many recognised at the time, was that the government simply had no legal power to do this. The Animal Health Act 1981 was quite specific. Animals could only be killed when they were either infected or had been directly exposed to infection. The whole point of the pre-emptive cull was that it was designed to kill animals which had not yet been exposed to the virus, to stop it spreading. The cull was thus a criminal act, on unprecedented scale.

This was where Janet Hughes was inspired to the course of action which is the story of her book. In July 2001, when the epidemic was already long past its peak, the Welsh Assembly decided to round up and slaughter 20,000 sheep on the Brecon Beacons. Janet describes how she bought a small flock of these sheep, to entitle her to challenge in the courts the legality of what the Assembly was proposing. She sank her entire life savings on a legal action in which it seemed she had both the law and truth on her side.

But then Kakfa took over. Janet describes how Maff (the Ministry of Agriculture, Fisheries and Food) in London became so worried by the implications of her action that it took over the case from the Welsh Assembly. She describes her bizarre encounters with lawyers and with the court system. She describes how, through tireless research, she came across a document which showed that Maff's chief vet had falsified the evidence in claiming that many of the sheep on the Brecon Beacons were diseased. But for reasons never properly explained, she was not allowed to produce this damning evidence in court. A judge in the London High Court dismissed her claim, and she ended up facing a bill for costs from Maff of £17,000.

It was a year later that I myself first picked up on Janet's story, following the ludicrous incident when two bailiffs arrived one morning at her home and prepared to remove her property, including the car she needed for her work and a toy jeep and quad bike belonging to her 12-year old son Matthew (whose support for his mother's stand had been one of her greatest sources of encouragement). This action by the 'Maffia' bailiffs went so far beyond what they were legally entitled to do that Janet's plight quickly blossomed into a cause celebre. Well-wishers sent money from all over the country. The bailiffs were forced to back down. Eventually a highly embarrassed ministry (now renamed Defra, widely known as the 'Department for the Elimination of Farming and Rural Affairs') agreed to settle for a mere £4000: the sum contributed by all those who had been horrified by Janet's story.

In September 2003 two law professors at Cardiff University, inspired by what Janet had done, produced a trenchant paper confirming that she was entirely correct in the point of law she had wanted to make. The government's culling policy was indeed illegal. In giving such supine support to the government, the courts had grievously blundered. I am delighted to introduce Janet's touching and chilling account of an episode which provides an invaluable epilogue to the story of that awful time. It was a drama which became a catastrophe – thanks to the incompetence of an arrogant, deceitful and corrupt government, as Janet's book so vividly brings home.

Christopher Booker

Introduction

Prior to 2001, those of us in farming, animal welfare and rural communities lived our lives, oblivious to the greater powers of this Country – for they had never touched our lives before.

This changed dramatically with the onset of the Foot and Mouth Disease outbreak when our government turned its back on its own people and forced through a policy of mass culling, allowing no one to stand in their way.

Blatant cruelty went on day by day as thousands of healthy and innocent animals were killed – many buried alive. It was not only sheep, cattle, goats and pigs on farms that were dealt this dreadful treatment, but also those treasured as family pets. Innocent law-abiding citizens were harassed, intimidated and scared witless by government agencies, the police and vets – the very people we thought we could trust and rely on.

Janet Hughes describes her story in this book. Unlike many of us who watched the KILLING PENS in the Brecon Beacons being set up and felt powerless to act, this brave and courageous lady immediately took action and prevented any further mass killing of the hefted sheep.

From there on life for Janet and her family would never be the same. Two years of legal battles commenced, culminating in Defra demanding costs of £17,000 and sending bailiffs, who threatened to remove all of her possessions and her son's toys. Her case eventually progressed to the European Court of Human Rights.

THE KILLING PENS is a documented history of one woman's fight against a corrupt and devious plan to eradicate our small farms. A strong deep belief that this wanton killing was wrong led to Janet being caught up in a world of lies and deceit and official cover-ups. This book is a memorial to all those animals who died needlessly under the guise of Foot and Mouth Disease and all those people who will never forget the horrendous suffering they witnessed and endured as the government of this Country relentlessly tore the very core out of the countryside.

Sue Burton, founder of Remus Memorial Sanctuary, Essex.

PART ONE

ROAD TO THE CASE

1

A Journey

21 August 2001, a date that will always remain etched into my memory. It was on this day that I sat in courtroom number 3, at the Royal Courts of Justice in London, embroiled in a legal battle that finally came to an end on 22 August 2003.

I was there with my son Matthew, who was eleven years old at the time, our friend Pat Innocent, a smallholder from Gloucestershire and Dafydd Morris, a farmer from Snowdonia. Matthew and I had travelled down the day before on the train from Shrewsbury and by the time we arrived in London night had fallen and it was dark. What struck us both was the feeling that we had reached some strange Soviet station in the grip of an icy winter. Huge clouds of steam bellowed from the engines and I would not have been at all surprised to see people wearing fur hats and scarves. It was all very far from re-assuring.

We had arrived much later than planned because our train had taken a detour and when we had arrived at Paddington instead of Euston it was getting on for about 10.30pm. The station was fairly busy with people milling about but it felt as if they were on the other side of a glass wall. Matthew was very tired and I was beginning to feel the strain of worrying about the next day. We had planned to meet Pat much earlier and go out for a meal but we now bought burgers and fries and went to sit down on a very hard, green metal bench opposite a man who stared at us as if we weren't there. I was trying to remain cheerful for Matthew's sake but we both shivered as we ate and began to long for our beds at the B&B. We ate up as quickly as we could and then went off to find the Underground. We bought a one way ticket to Victoria station and the swirling hot air of the dimly lit platform warmed us uncomfortably as we waited for the tube.

When we eventually reached the Enrico Hotel in Warwick Way, we were handed a message that Pat had left for us. It was by now far too late to let her know that we had arrived and I wished so much that she was staying at the same hotel as us. She had booked into a different place in the same street because this one had not had another room available. I felt utterly wretched and just wanted to go back home. We were provided with a key and given instructions as to where our room was and we searched for it up miles of metal stair-ways with automatic lights, which kept switching on and off at just the wrong moment. Glyn, my partner and Matthew's Dad, had stayed to look after our several cats and dogs at our cottage back in Mid-Wales, and as soon as we closed the door to the room we rang him to let him know that we were okay and had arrived safely. Then after a quick wash Matthew and I sank into the sagging beds and tried to sleep.

I lay awake for a long while wondering what I had done. The next day, a Tuesday, loomed ahead and I felt that it would be a day on which a decision would be made that would seal the fate of thousands of sheep, and other farm animals. The hearing at the Royal Courts of Justice had been ordered the week before on 16 August. It was a hearing at which I was going to request permission to apply for a judicial review against the Governments of Wales and England, for their senseless slaughter of many thousands of healthy sheep on the Brecon Beacons under the guise of eradicating Foot and Mouth Disease, (FMD).

I went over and over what had led us to this point in time, remaining convinced that the hearing the next day was crucial and part of a process that had to happen. There were many folk who would have been better equipped than I but no-one else would make a move so I had taken it upon myself to tackle the National Assembly for Wales, (NAW), and inadvertently, the Department of the Environment Food and Rural Affairs, (DEFRA). Maybe no one else was as naive or as stupid.

2

The Court

It was a bright sunny morning. Mercifully, the night had not been completely sleepless for me. I stirred Matthew awake. He had slept quite soundly and I was very glad, as I knew he would find the day ahead very tiring. We washed and dressed then went down for breakfast. The hotel still seemed drab but much more cheerful than the night before. We followed the sound of clattering dishes and chatter, and found the room for breakfast. This room felt quite different from the rest of the hotel, as if it had put on its make up for the world. We sat at a small round table. A girl, who struck me as Greek, came to ask if we wanted tea or coffee and there was a menu for choice of breakfast. Matthew and I whispered to one another about all sorts of things including the hearing. I poured the tea and remember feeling fairly optimistic. Surely the judge would rule in our favour having ordered a hearing so quickly? We just had to win and make it safe for all the sheep still alive and well in the Brecon Beacons National Park.

The media had become interested and supportive over the past few weeks and two radio stations wanted interviews before we set off to court. There was a woman who did an interview for Radio Wales and a man from Radio Shropshire. Both wanted to know how I felt the hearing would go. I told them that it all depended on whether the judge felt able to rule against the Government. In between the interviews Pat arrived at the hotel. At last I was able to let her know what had happened the previous evening and why we had not been able to meet up with her. Pat was as nervous as I was, if not more, and we all went up to our room for a quick chat. She had brought with her a testing kit, which she had used when her sheep were under threat from a cull in the Forest of Dean, and wanted to know if it might be useful evidence. I didn't know as I had no idea what DEFRA's evidence would be, but it was very interesting to see how the test had revealed that her sheep were all healthy. Pat had been threatened for several weeks by vets and officials from the Ministry but she had survived, as had all her sheep, thanks to support from her solicitor, neighbours and the media.

After sorting out where to leave our bags for the day we set off to catch a bus to the Royal Courts of Justice in the Strand. We watched the sights from the double-decker. A short while later we were walking towards the court. I could see Bryn Thomas waiting for us. He is a clerk at the firm of solicitors in Cardiff who were acting for me then and is one of the people who I shall remember with a great deal of warmth. His parents farm in Carmarthenshire so he understood why I felt so emotive about the case. It mattered to him too.

The entrance to the Royal Courts of Justice is vast and wonderful. We shook hands with Bryn and introduced Pat, then nervously went up the steps and on inside through into the hall. I was not allowed to take my camera in, so Bryn dashed off to a shop across the road where they keep cameras for the day, for people appearing at court. When Bryn returned we walked through the hall and up some stairs through to a dark corridor with alcoves along it. In one of the alcoves sat my barrister, Guy Adams, at a table loaded with various books and documents. He had travelled down from Bristol that morning.

It was then that I looked at the evidence from DEFRA for the first time. I had not been able to read it before as it had been faxed through to the solicitor the previous evening. We had waited at home for as long as possible the day before, in the hope that it would come through before we set off. The train to London had been delayed and I had phoned Mr Wilkins, the solicitor, from Shrewsbury station. He had told me that the evidence had just come through and that there was a lot of it. DEFRA had refused to provide details of test results and whether there had been any live FMD virus in the sheep that had been culled on the Brecon Beacons in late July/early August; I wondered what evidence lay in store for us.

We sat down at the table next to Guy Adams and Bryn handed me the wad of evidence. I then caught sight of Dafydd, the farmer who had come to support us. He had come down the previous day too and had attended a demonstration outside the Ministry. It turned out that he had collapsed and had been taken to hospital. He had been discharged and had found a hotel for the night and had then made his way to the courts. I felt proud that a farmer wanted to be there with us. I had first met him earlier in the summer, at a meeting in the Town Hall in Welshpool, our local market town, when Richard North, a researcher in the European Parliament, had come to speak to the farmers.

As I talked with Dafydd I managed some glances at the evidence, but as soon as I had begun to gain any sense of it we were called to go into court. We had to rush because we were late apparently and before we could all arrange ourselves along the bench in came the judge. Here was the person who would determine the fate of the sheep. What was he like? Did he like animals? He looked quite nice; ordinary and not too stuck up.

Dafydd sat behind us, and Matthew and Pat were on either side of me so I felt very safe. Bryn sat beyond Pat with his large notebook. I felt like a criminal, which was stupid of me, but it was as if I was about to be judged along with the sheep. The room was a proper old-fashioned courtroom as you see on television dramas, with a very large old clock high on one wall and windows that kept the day out. There were quite a number of people in the room and it took me a while to feel comfortable enough to start studying them.

There were some people to our right with files of documents in front of them so it seemed as if there were legal folk there on behalf of either DEFRA or the Welsh Assembly. There was a man with a very red face who looked embarrassed and beyond him a woman who did not look very nice at all. She was already grinning at something and that made me very angry inside. In front of her there were two barristers with their wigs jigging about. They looked as if they had come to have a laugh. There was a third barrister, round-faced and looking very serious. This seemed like a whole load of trouble for Guy, one barrister against three of the opposition.

3

Outbreak

Over the past two years several people have asked me how I became involved with fighting to save the sheep of the Brecon Beacons, as the area is a long way from where we live. For the answer you have to know what happened to thousands of farm animals in Powys from February through to July 2001.

At the end of February we had visited Cardiff for a couple of days, and had met two women staying at the hotel, who were from Snowdonia in North Wales. At breakfast, as we chatted, the women told us that a farmer near to where they lived had sheep wintered on Anglesey and was in danger of losing them because foot and mouth disease had apparently been found on the island on 27 February. The women were appalled that the only 'cure' for foot and mouth seemed to be slaughter. We all agreed that animals should be nursed back to health.

On 1 March, St David's Day, Matthew and I drove out into the countryside around Cardiff whilst waiting for Glyn to complete a course related to his work. The thought of foot and mouth being on Anglesey had cast a slight shadow on the sunny day, but not for one moment could I have imagined the change to our countryside that was due to take place. That night we drove back home, up through the Brecon Beacons. The roads were treacherous with ice and snow; a few solitary mountain sheep grazed at the side of the road in the cold and the lonely darkness.

When we reached home we had a chat with the pet-minder, who had taken care of our cats and dogs. He too had heard about foot and mouth having arrived in Wales. The news was not good, but I was just glad to be back home.

A couple of weeks after returning from Cardiff, we were driving to our local town of Montgomery when we saw a woman in white overalls standing on the verge by the hedge of a farm called The Ditches. A little further on there was a notice with red lettering on it. It was a Ministry of Agriculture Fisheries and Food notice, bearing the awful words of 'Foot and Mouth Disease. Keep Out.' Stupidly, I had thought that it was not possible for it to have reached a place so close to us.

On 11 March, all 228 dairy cattle from the farm were slaughtered; 4 of them had apparently shown illness. Links with Welshpool market, so wrongly assumed to have been a factor in the spread of disease, were disproved, but officialdom was to keep referring to the market link for months to come.

Over the coming weeks the situation grew worse. Four farms near to The Ditches, became identified as infected premises, and lost their livestock. It was all becoming dreadfully worrying.

On Saturday, 24 March the situation finally hit home. There is a farm called The Brickyard only about 50 yards down the road from us, where all was thought to be well with their animals, but they had been worried as some of their land bordered on The Ditches farm. On Wednesday, 21 March, I had spoken on the telephone with Hilda, the farmer's wife, and she said that so far all their animals were okay and some of the ewes had started lambing. In a few days they were going to bring most of the ewes over the main road to the lambing shed near the house.

Three days later, on Saturday morning, the phone rang. Hilda, who brought us Christmas swedes each year and always used to be so cheerful, was in tears. She explained that the Ministry had told them they were a dangerous contact and that all their sheep and cattle had to be destroyed. The men had started carrying the ewes over the road to kill them in the shed and Hilda had drawn the curtains to shut it all out. I was totally shocked. I told her that they did not have to agree to this. She went to tell Michael, her husband, but he had decided that the experts knew best, as he later said to me on the phone. They lost their herd of cattle and all their large flock of sheep and lambs, some born, many still unborn in their mothers. Subsequently all their animals were found to have been healthy and had posed no threat whatsoever. The manipulative tactic of telling them that they had to allow their own animals to go in order to safeguard neighbouring farms had worked, and this tactic was to be used repeatedly with many other farmers across the UK.

It was Matthew's 11th birthday on the coming Monday, 26 March, and we had to do some last minute shopping. As we left we could see several vehicles down the road parked outside the farm and the road was closed. We walked around Toys R Us in Shrewsbury that Saturday trying to be cheerful and chose some surprises for Matthew. I prayed that the sheep would be spared and that they were not killing them. The men would have left and gone away; this was all a bad dream. We bought a little remote control car for Matthew together with a few other things and I tried to put out of mind what might be happening back in the village. When we got home we knew the nightmare had been all too real. The vehicles were still parked outside the farm, and they had started to cart the dead animals back over the road to be put on a pyre in one of the fields further down the road. I made sure that I hardly glanced again in that direction until the machinery had gone away.

On 26 March, Matthew's birthday, they started to burn the animals. We were in the kitchen. Matthew was playing with his new remote control car and chasing our whippet, Daisy, with it, when we started to smell a dreadful stench that I hope I will never smell again. The smell permeated the kitchen and in vain we tried to keep it out by closing all the windows. We went outside and looked down the road, where smoke was heaving its way up from the field beyond the farm. It was a terrible sight.

Over the next weeks the smell became more intense, as more and more animals from surrounding farms were slaughtered and burnt. It felt like being stranded in the middle of a very evil place with the smell of death all around. We kept the windows closed for weeks but the smell still came in. Each time that I went out into the garden I felt physically sick. Also I was struck by the silence. The birds had stopped singing and there was no longer any dawn-chorus. The countryside seemed to be dying at the hands of evil doers and the sweet air of spring had been turned into the acrid stench of Hell.

On 23 March, Professor David King, a chemist and Tony Blair's Chief Scientist, had announced that the Government was introducing the 'contiguous cull' policy, based on a mathematical model drawn up by a team from Imperial College, led by Professor Roy Anderson, a zoologist. The sound of this new policy made me shudder. Animals on farms deemed to be infected premises would be slaughtered within 24 hours and those on contiguous farms would be slaughtered within 48 hours. There did not seem to be any mention of waiting for test results; only a mad rush to kill on a massive scale.

A couple of days after Matthew's birthday the then President of the Farmers' Union of Wales made an announcement on the tea-time news that caused all three of us to wonder if we had heard correctly. Mr Bob Parry stated that there was to be a contiguous cull in the Churchstoke area. There had been four farms diagnosed as infected premises to our knowledge, along the road to Montgomery, some 4 miles away, but suddenly there was to be a contiguous cull, which would mean that all livestock within three kilometres of each 'infected' farm would be killed. It was horrifying and we hoped that we had misheard.

The 3km zones were meant to be protection zones; not killing zones. As noted by Christopher Booker in The Sunday Telegraph on 22 April 2001,

'These 'three kilometre zones' are specified by EU directive 85/511, which dictates much of how the Ministry of Agriculture, Fisheries and Food (Maff) is handling the epidemic; but the decision to 'ring cull' all animals in these zones was a refinement devised by our own officials'.

A mass cull of sheep was taking place on Anglesey around this time, resulting in many pyres and a mass burial site on the island. I had been in contact with a group of smallholders, who had refused to have their sheep killed. They became known as the Anglesey Six. MAFF attempted legal proceedings against them, but towards the end of April withdrew their application for an injunction. On Friday, 27 April, vets apparently found FMD symptoms in two sheep on one of the group's smallholdings. All their animals were slaughtered on Sunday, 29 April. This particular smallholder, Mike Lowe, had bravely aired his views against the cull on television, and had received great condemnation from Bob Parry, interviewed alongside him. The subsequent slaughter of this smallholder's sheep seemed to me like revenge for daring to attack the cull policy in public. Test results proved negative.

The initial outbreak (one lamb) in an abattoir on Anglesey had resulted in thirteen premises being declared infected. However, it later transpired that only five of those had actually tested positive for FMD. The number of dangerous contact farms that lost their livestock was staggering; some one hundred or more premises were 'taken out'. The majority of them were not tested, but of those that were, only one returned a positive test result, which was for antibodies, not virus. 47,000 healthy sheep from the south-west corner of Anglesey were pre-emptively culled in the massacre.

The apparent ignorance of the authorities, including the State Veterinary Service, with regards to basic science continued to baffle me. Animals with antibodies, the immune defence against disease, were being slaughtered on a massive scale. The reason for the killing of these healthy animals was unfathomable.

4

Meetings

On Sunday 1 April there was a meeting in Welshpool at a hotel called the Royal Oak. The meeting had apparently been arranged secretly and was supposed to be closed to the public, although we did not know that at the time. News of it came trickling through the community. A local farmer who was intent on keeping his animals told me about it on the phone on the Saturday. He had heard that Carwyn Jones, the Welsh Assembly Minister for Rural Affairs, was to be there. We decided to go to it.

When we arrived at the Royal Oak there were lots of people there. There were television crews with cameras ready for action. There were farmers and dealers, county councillors and local vets, all gathered in the yard clumped together in various groups of intense discussion. We stood next to a chap who turned out to be an organic farmer from about 10 miles away. He was most concerned and critical of how FMD was being tackled and held a file of fact-sheets and blank paper for notes.

After about half an hour the door to the conference room opened and a few people filed out. A man then came out and we could see him discussing something with people who stood near the doorway. One of the people was Glyn Davies, a local farmer and also a member of the Welsh Assembly. He was not looking very pleased. An announcement was then made that the next meeting was not supposed to be an open one. You could feel that there was a great deal of anger about to erupt. The man, whoever he was, then quickly announced that people could however go in and there was an immediate rush towards the entrance.

We found an empty row of chairs and sat down. The room filled up and lots of people remained standing at the back. The various officials returned to their seats at the top table. We saw that the First Minister, Rhodri

Morgan, was amongst those who were making the visit to our main local market town. Next to Rhodri Morgan sat Carwyn Jones. Apparently both of them had been helicoptered down from Anglesey. Our MP, Lembit Opik, was there too, managing to look jolly and serious at the same time. Someone stood up and asked for quiet, and then explained again that this was not meant to have been a meeting open to the public. Anger immediately rose to the surface and people began shouting questions at the Ministers, who had begun to look very uneasy.

The main impression that we had of the Ministers at that meeting was that they seemed unable to speak about anything other than death, reasons for killing the animals, best ways of transporting the dead animals and how they were dealing with environmental problems from the disposal of dead animals.

Several people wanted to ask questions. They were asked to stand up then give their name and where they lived. One of the local vets said that he was concerned about the welfare of the animals and that he felt this factor was not being taken into account by the Ministry or anyone involved in the process. This was strongly denied by Carwyn Jones. Both Matthew and I wanted to ask questions. Heart pounding, I put up my hand. Someone asked me to stand up and give my name and address, which I did. I put my question. I asked why it was acceptable for trucks of dead animals to be transported through Powys and yet ewes were not allowed to be moved a few yards over the road to lamb. Carwyn Jones answered, staring most of the time at the ceiling. He said that the trucks carrying the dead animals were sealed and that no waste products leaked. My feeling was that this was no answer to my question at all.

Mr Jones was heckled on this point, as it was well known that trucks had been leaking animal fluids across many roads in Wales, and I mentioned this fact. Rhodri Morgan told me angrily to 'shush' and I was not allowed to have that point, or my original question, addressed. Carwyn Jones repeated his monologue about sealed trucks. The room became full of angry shouting people waving their fists at the Ministers; one chap across the aisle jumped up and down with frustration. At that moment I felt that it would have been great to have had a riot because the Ministers needed a good shake up. However, all that happened was that Rhodri Morgan stood up and threatened that unless people quietened down the meeting would end and everyone would have to leave. Matthew, very bravely, told the Ministers, 'You keep saying that if vaccination takes place the export trade will stop, but won't the export trade stop anyway now that foot and mouth is in Britain?' Several folk clapped, and the Ministers had no answers.

The meeting lasted about an hour and a half, with the discussion always being steered back by the Ministers to how best to deal with dead animals and how to manage the killing on a mass scale. To me they acted like people who were under an evil spell.

I was glad when the meeting ended. We talked with a girl who I had been in school with, who is a part-time shepherd. She did not know what to make of it all either. With her there were two other women, Ammara and Michaela. Ammara carried a bunch of white flowers as a symbol of peace; she believed that spiritual wickedness was at the heart of what was happening to the animals. It did feel like that. Michaela had been sitting in front of me and had heard me mention that we were going down to London to a demonstration outside the Ministry headquarters in Smith Square. She said that she would like to come too.

We left the Royal Oak and walked to the car. Close behind us was the man who had been jumping up and down. He waved so we went over and introduced ourselves. His name is Arwyn and his wife, Elaine, was with him. They farm near Welshpool. How this mess was going to end, he said, he did not know, but he was convinced it was a plot. Elaine agreed with him, and so did we. Ammara waved to us and left, still carrying her white flowers of peace.

The following day, Monday 2 April, I went with Matthew to Welshpool again, to a meeting of a few folk who had formed an organisation called Unity. It was mainly composed of a couple of local farmers, one of whom was the local representative of the Farmers' Union of Wales, FUW, and several concerned local people. The meeting was held in a little room at the back of a solicitor's office. On the wall was a large map of the area, which reminded me of something out of a war film because it had little red markers on the places where FMD had been diagnosed. It was like a map showing where the enemy might strike next.

Not much happened at the meeting. The FUW man listened to a tape, which no one else was able to hear. It was from a meeting of some officials and was apparently very important but I never found out what it was about. The other farmer came in a bit later. He was very cross and wanted action of some kind. When he heard that we were going down to London with Michaela the following day, he said that he wanted us to go to the National Farmers' Union, (NFU), head office in Shaftesbury Avenue. He seemed adamant about this but I had no idea what we could achieve by going there. However, we said that we would.

We stayed behind for a while talking with Michaela. She is from South Africa and has lived near Montgomery for around 10 years. She keeps a few Ryeland sheep and she was extremely worried as vets were testing at the farms next to her smallholding, which is situated along the road to Montgomery not far from the initial outbreak in the dairy herd at The Ditches. We were all of the opinion that something quite sinister was going on and that there was some hidden motive behind it all.

A bizarre deal that was apparently being offered by MAFF was that if farmers gave up their sheep they would be allowed to keep their cattle. Three farmers near to The Ditches farm were to agree to such a deal. What was it that was so offensive about the sheep that they had to be killed and the cattle spared? Nothing seemed to make sense any longer.

We arranged to meet the next day, then drove home. As we came nearer home we could see smoke pouring across the wide valley from one of the farms which borders our village. At the weekend they had given in to the slaughter of hundreds of perfectly healthy ewes and lambs. We drove on and I noticed that a farmer was in the fields below checking his sheep. I turned the car round a little way on, and went back in the hope of speaking with him to see how his animals were faring. We found a shallow lay-by, and I stood on the bank and watched him weave his way between his flock. He was carrying his shepherd's crook, which seemed like a sign of goodness in a land that was filling with an almost tangible sense of dread.

As he went further and further down the fields I gave up hope of speaking with him. I turned round to get back in the car and looking over the road, saw that a large group of sheep was watching me. They had come right up to the hedge and started calling, almost as if they were crying. Matthew leaned out of the car window. I began to talk with them and realised that they were full of panic. The smell of smoke was drifting over to them and they knew it was from their kindred. This notion might seem ridiculous but I know for sure that they knew what was happening to their own kind. A truck came past. The sheep ran away up the field but then came back to the hedge again. I made a promise to them that I would try to stop it all and make sure they would be kept safe.

A week or so later white trucks appeared on the verge near their field and we didn't see them again. I feared the worst. However, over the following months I tried to keep my promise to them.

5

Warning

When we arrived home from Welshpool I made a cup of tea and then went upstairs to sort out clothes for us for the next day. During the last few weeks I had been looking on the internet for information on FMD and had found a web site called Sheepdrove organised by a large organic farming enterprise in southern England. The owner of the farm is Peter Kindersley, the man who founded the publishers, Dorling Kindersley.

Peter Kindersley had challenged MAFF at the end of March in the High Court, and had been granted leave to apply for a judicial review of the culling policy. Then suddenly he had dropped the case on 2 April. He was to be at the demonstration and I wanted to find out why he had stopped the legal action.

The phone rang. It was a policeman from the local station in Newtown, who said he wanted to come to see me. I had absolutely no idea why a policeman should have the need to visit us and I told him that it was not convenient, as I was busy preparing for an early start the next day. He insisted that he had to come to see me, which made me defensive. I did not want a policeman coming round so I asked him if he could explain what the problem was on the phone. He agreed. Apparently someone had made a complaint that I was causing trouble locally. I was taken aback and asked if he could tell me the name of the person who had made this complaint, which in my opinion was completely unjustified and false. He said that he was not able to tell me the person's name but that they were local. I then quickly tried to think of people who I had spoken with recently.

Over the previous fortnight, I had spoken with several local farmers and one of them had not liked the fact that I was asking about whether or not their animals had been tested before being destroyed. I had spoken with the wife of a farmer who also worked on a neighbouring farm. I had asked her if their test results had been positive and she had told me that she did not know but that their animals had indeed had FMD. A short while later another farmer had phoned up and his tone was not friendly. He started accusing me of poking my nose in where it was not wanted and became fairly belligerent. He said that I had better watch it or else he would report me. The complaint would have caused me more distress had I not known that he was the son of a farmer with whom I had had an unintentional dispute several years previously.

The dispute had concerned a letter that I had written to the local paper about an ancient hedge that had been removed. I had not even realised that my letter had become printed and worse still that it had been awarded letter of the week. The first I knew of it was when I received a phone call from this man's father, who rented the farm where the hedge had been destroyed. He had congratulated me on my letter in a very odd tone and had then launched into a diatribe against me. The dispute had never been amicably resolved. The farmer had made statements to the press, and had demanded that I visit his farm. I never did this because he had sounded so aggressive and hostile. So the attitude of this farmer did not come as a great surprise to me, but nonetheless it was quite dismaying to realise that my attempts of help had been turned into the actions of a troublemaker.

I asked the policeman if the person concerned happened to be a farmer who lived locally. The policeman hinted that 'yes this could be the case'. I then explained to him that all I had been doing was phoning up local farmers, in the possibly naive hope that I could help in some way and so prevent them losing their livestock. The policeman then seemed to realise that I was not in fact someone who was causing trouble.

'Miss Hughes, you had better be very careful who you speak with in future.'

This sounded like a stern, but sympathetic, warning and I never rang local farmers again. However, they were not the only ones whose lives were to become affected by FMD in Powys over the next months and the policeman's warning went to the back of my mind.

6

Trip to London

The next morning, Tuesday 3 April, Michaela came to pick us up at 8am. The sun was shining and the sky was a bright blue; Easter was approaching. When we got in the car she was on her mobile speaking with her husband. I thought that a bit strange, as she must have only just left home. She was speaking in a matter of fact way, yet at the same time, sounded terribly worried and the conversation hinged on their sheep at home. She told him to keep the padlocks on the gate and not to let anyone in. When she came off the phone her words filled me with horror. Ministry vets and officials had apparently made the decision to slaughter all livestock from all the farms along the road to Montgomery. So here was the predicted contiguous cull.

Apparently another farm not far from The Ditches had been declared an infected premises the day before. There were a large number of farms that fell within the contiguous cull area and one farmer had tried in vain to blockade his drive. He had put his tractor and other vehicles across it, but he had been forced to comply. Michaela said that he had even been made to get his sheep dog to round up the ewes and lambs.

Michaela drove fairly fast, speaking now and again to her husband. The tension in the car was almost intolerable. Here she was coming with us to London when it sounded as if she should be back at home. I asked her if she wanted to turn round and go back. Matthew and I would not mind. No, she said that she still wanted to come with us, so we continued our journey to Shrewsbury. I felt full of panic. It was too beautiful a day for this horror to be happening.

We arrived in Shrewsbury at 9am and there was just time to buy a newspaper before boarding the train for London. One of the articles in the newspaper was about FMD. A Masai tribesman had written to the UK government offering to help with curative treatment for the animals. He and his people were appalled at what was happening over here. I wonder if he ever received a reply.

When we arrived at Euston it was already 12.20 pm, and the demo had been due to start at noon. I rushed to the Ladies. When I returned Michaela was back on the phone to her husband. The animals were being killed at all the neighbouring farms and he was worried that he would not be able to keep the officials at bay. Michaela said something that became lost in the noise of the packed station, then ran off and disappeared towards the escalators. We assumed that she had decided to go back home.

By now the demonstration outside MAFF Headquarters had become insignificant. I did not know quite where to turn or what to do. Matthew followed me outside the station. I phoned Glyn and told him how awful things were down the road back home. He didn't know where to turn either. I then got out the London guide and found the telephone number of Buckingham Palace. I rang the number and spoke with a woman in the press office there who must have thought that I was deranged. I explained what was happening back in our wonderful Mid-Wales, but she sounded as if she could not understand what I was trying to tell her at all. No, it was not possible to speak with any member of the Royal family, and no it was not possible to make any appointment at any time in the future came the clear message.

When I look back I realise that what I was doing must have seemed crazy and I knew that it was, but I felt desperate. HRH Prince Charles, Prince of Wales, surely he could find a way to stop this hideous activity? The impenetrable wall of propriety came down in front of me, and as some pigeons came strutting round our feet, I realised how foolish I had been to try to contact a real person at that institution. The Queen could not have helped even had she known about my plea on the telephone.

Anyway, what power could I have had when a world-renowned expert in FMD, Professor Fred Brown, had offered to meet the Prime Minister and had been turned away? Professor Brown had defined the virus in the 1950's and had worked at the Animal Health Institute at Pirbright, Surrey for many years. He was in his late 70's but still worked at that time as a visiting professor for the US Department of Agriculture in their laboratories at Plum Island, Greenport, on Long Island, New York.

The way in which the UK Government was spurning expert advice and opinion, whilst relying on the computer modelling team from Imperial College, beggared belief. None of the scientists in the team, one of whom was a mathematician, were experts on FMD and they had created a computer model of the spread of the disease based on what is now known to be spurious theoretical information. It was this model that led to the destruction of around 10 million healthy farm animals during what can only be described as the animal holocaust of 2001.

7

Meeting Theo

As we turned to leave the station we saw Michaela running up to us. She'd been looking for us. I told her that we had thought that she had decided to return home. No, she was still coming to the demo; there was nothing that she felt she could achieve by getting back on a train immediately. Things back home would have to be sorted out by her husband. So we left the station and walked to Smith Square, past Big Ben and the Houses of Parliament. People with placards and black dress were walking towards us, a few at a time, and we realised that they were probably people who had been to the demo, which must be over by now.

We turned the corner into Smith Square. There were leaflets strewn on the ground and a small group of people with boards leant against walls. The demo did seem to have ended. There was a chap draped with a Union Jack and a few other folk, who were chatting to one another. We walked towards them and I recognised Peter Kindersley and his wife. We introduced ourselves and explained that our train had been late. I asked him why he had stopped his legal action. He said the case had made the Government listen. The Government would now look at alternatives, including vaccination and he did not want to get in the way of Government policy. I did not consider it likely that the Government would consider vaccination and could not help feeling fairly angry. His wife said that they were going to a pub and asked us if we wanted to join them. I quite sharply told them that I had not come all the way down to London to go to a pub.

By this time, someone else had joined us. He was standing to my right side and he seemed to be listening intently. He introduced himself as Theo and wanted to know all about everyone, where we were from, and why we were all there. Theo was against all sorts of animal cruelty and had been to several recent protests in Somerset, where he lived. He wanted to find out how to organise protests at farm gates when the officials were using force to gain access to farms. I noticed that he kept looking round as if to check something and he said that the surveillance camera in a van nearby was probably being used to keep track on him. It transpired that he was an environmental activist, who had taken part in many contentious demonstrations for various environmental issues. He was apparently well known to the Government and had taken part in another demonstration some time ago outside the MAFF Headquarters. I began to feel nervous and as if the camera was watching me too.

I told Theo that we had planned to go to the NFU Head Office. He said that he would like to come along too. So, we said our goodbyes to the very few folk left by the banners and started to walk to a tube station for a train that would take us to Shaftesbury Avenue. Theo said that he knew the way to the tube station we needed, but we did need to consult my London map at many stages. Michaela walked in front with Theo whilst Matthew and I trailed behind. Matthew grew more and more tired as Theo and Michaela seemed to walk faster and faster. We went past Big Ben and the Houses of Parliament again but Matthew did not seem to view them with the same interest as before.

Michaela was talking intently to Theo as we tried to keep up with them. He turned round to check that we were still behind and I had to yell to them to slow down because they were walking too fast for Matthew to keep up, or me for that matter. We reached Charing Cross station and the claustrophobic atmosphere hit me as we went through to look at the map on the wall to check which route we needed. It was very hot and very busy. We went to buy our tickets then headed for the escalator. When Matthew was a toddler he had slipped badly on an escalator at a shopping precinct in Shrewsbury and had been too nervous to try them again ever since. I told Theo this quietly as I could sense that Matthew was becoming apprehensive. Very calmly Theo went down the escalator first. When he got to the bottom he turned round and smiled up at Matthew. I shall always remember the smile and outstretched arms as if to make Matthew safe. Matthew walked onto the steps and down. I followed. We took a tube to Leicester Square, then walked out into the streets in search of the NFU offices.

After a fairly lengthy walk we reached a part of Shaftesbury Avenue that had numbers near to those of the NFU offices. As we took in the various buildings it seemed that none of them matched the type for the offices of a farming union. We thought that we had found them but the offices turned out to be some other large enterprise. Then we spotted it across the road; a large building of red brick with the NFU symbol above the entrance. We went up to the glass doors and followed one another in.

8

Chilled Milk

Ahead of us was a large reception desk where a woman sat watching us approach. We all went up to the desk and Theo explained to her that we had come to speak with someone about Foot and Mouth Disease if at all possible. She looked at each of us in a fairly dismissive way but said that she would try to find someone who would have time to speak with us. She motioned us towards a sofa and we sat in a row, except for Theo, who stood and talked with us quietly whilst glancing out of the large smoked glass windows onto the busy street. There was a fresh milk drinks dispenser, and Matthew and I helped ourselves to cartons of chilled milk. It felt like the only sign that we were in the offices of a farming organisation. There were some NFU brochures on the table. I picked one up and put it in my bag.

A short while later an elderly man came in pushing a trolley bag in front of him. He went up to the desk and we could hear him tell the woman that he had come to see Ben Gill, the president of the NFU. We listened intently. The woman told him that someone would come down shortly to speak with him. The old man came and sat near us and a little while later a fair-haired girl came to tell him that unfortunately Mr Gill was not able to see him as he had gone somewhere in a helicopter. She would, however, she said, try to find someone else to speak with him.

The old man turned to us. I will never forget our strange conversation. He told us that he was a professor of science from Czechoslovakia. We told him that we had come to the NFU head office in the hope that we might gain some information about the FMD outbreak. He asked where we were from and when I mentioned Wales he seemed to grow more earnest. He started talking about the war between Israel and Palestine and said that in a way Wales was in a similar situation to Israel. His eyes were intensely dark

I noticed and I felt as if he could see all our fears about what was happening over FMD. I said that in Israel they treated their animals better and he then said, speaking directly to me: 'You'll never win you know' as if he knew already that I was going to fight something, 'and do you know why?' I said I didn't know. What he then said chilled me to the bone.

Michaela and Theo were immersed in their own conversation and had not taken much notice of what the old man had been saying but I felt very cold inside at what he had just told me. Our conversation trailed off. A chap came down from an office above to speak with the professor and they went off to another area of the large foyer.

Theo started talking about the World Trade Organisation and how all that had a lot to do with what was going on in the countryside. He seemed very buoyant. I felt too gloomy as I drank the rest of the cold milk. A few minutes later a tall dark-haired man came towards us and said that he understood that we had come to discuss something with him. He smiled, shook hands with us all and asked us to follow him. Up some steps we walked, past a canteen and I saw the old man at one of the tables. He had papers spread in front of him and as we walked past I stopped to ask him if I could have his contact details. He took out a small book and handed me a tiny label with his name and address on it. He seemed somehow bemused that I should ask him for it but at the same time I felt that he knew why. Later I noticed that his name was a very English name and realised that he must have had to change it at some stage, perhaps during the war. To this day I have not contacted him and I do not know why. Perhaps he has some answers to the questions that have arisen over the last two years but some disquiet has always prevented me from writing to him.

The tall man led us through the foyer and on into a quiet room with a large conference-type table taking up most of the space. I needed the loo and rushed off only to become lost in the corridors. Eventually Matthew found me and led me back the very short distance to the room with the huge table, where discussion had already begun. I sat down in the empty chair next to the man, who introduced himself and said that he would give us as much time as he had available. Michaela was talking about what was happening back in our area and I tried quickly to become part of the conversation. I said that I was very concerned indeed about the fact that so many animals were being culled. The man, a senior official, then appeared to realise that I was a part of the conversation. He said that yes what was happening was 'brutal'. He used this adjective several times during the course of the conversation. He told us that on the TV he was seeing friends in Cumbria having to give up their animals and he found this troubling. However, this brutal action was necessary in order to rid the country of FMD.

For several weeks I had been troubled by a terrible dread that the ongoing culling was going to result in the removal of the national sheep flock. Perhaps it had been the relentless fashion by which the culling had taken place that had caused this fear, or maybe it was the continual talk of the need to find more burial pits across the country that made me feel a total dread of what might take place. Whatever the reason, I had to ask this man. I asked him. He looked at me in completely straight fashion and said that this might happen. He was unperturbed at my reaction. He told us that there was the probability that at least 10 per cent of the national sheep flock would be lost. This was fact. This was inevitable from his tone. He said that they were prepared to slaughter the entire national flock in order to eradicate the disease. His words were horrifying and confirmed my worst fears.

Matthew said that if they kept killing sheep there would be none left. The man explained that if this did happen then there were many other countries from where more supplies of sheep would become available. I said to him that we were dealing with a curable virus; not the plague. This statement caused him to look at me in such a way that I cannot describe but it gave me time to see the tired redness of his eyes. He said nothing in response.

He told us that for each farm diagnosed with FMD around five other farms would be 'taken out'. This apparently was a model from the 1967 outbreak. It did not sound as if any lessons had been learned from that. A knock came on the door and the woman from the reception desk looked in. She told the official that he was to be at a meeting shortly. He said he wouldn't be long. The conversation resumed. He seemed intent on continuing. He told us that after the outbreak there would a radical restructuring of farming in Britain. There would be a change in the type of farming. 'There will be fewer farms. There will be larger farms and the smaller farms will be gone. There will be less sheep. There are too many sheep and they have to go.' The way in which he spoke made it all sound like a most definite plan. The room felt extremely cold and I felt dismayed at the attitude of this man sat next to me.

Michaela was very insistent that he listen to what was happening back home, and she wanted to be given answers about vaccination. So did I. The woman from reception returned. The official was required at the meeting. He told her again that he would not be long and I was very surprised that he did not call a halt to the discussion. We were very insignificant people in the world of farming and of commerce, and yet this man was giving us time that seemed to be encroaching on the time of other, more influential people. Theo later remarked how amazing he had found this point too. Michaela asked him about the possibility of vaccination of rare breeds and he was fairly dismissive even of this possibility. He said that it might be considered an option but he seemed totally unconcerned about the prospect of losing our rare breeds.

The meeting was brought to a fairly abrupt conclusion in the end, and it seemed to come about from my asking if there was a chance of a discussion on vaccination in the near future. The man seemed to take on a completely different aura after this remark. His face grew red with anger and he informed us that we had been very fortunate, to have been given so much of his time. We had come in 'off the street' and he was not normally inclined to give interviews to people under those circumstances. Theo was very appreciative and thanked him. I realised that my request had caused a great deal of anger. The official informed us that there was not the possibility of any discussion on vaccination. He said that he was now required at a meeting. We quickly thanked him for his time. Vaccination was obviously a taboo word at the NFU.

We left the building and I realised that I had left behind one of my bags. I walked back in and went to see if it was in the area where we had had the discussion. It wasn't there and as I came back through towards the foyer I saw that I had left it by the sofa where we'd sat with the professor. A feeling of being watched made me glance over to the lift door and the same official was waiting for the lift. He was looking at me in a curious manner, as if he didn't quite know what to make of me. He smiled and I said goodbye. Afterwards I thought how different he looked from when he had spoken with us; much older and slightly slumped, as if a burden was quietly weighing on him.

9

The Crying Lady

As we all headed back for the tube station we talked about what the NFU official had told us. All of us were very surprised at how much time he had given us, and how frank he had been with us. What he had said was extremely worrying, particularly in respect of the national flock. Theo said that he was going to try to meet up with a friend in London, so was now going to take a different route from us. He is a musician and had been carrying round a CD of music by his group; *'Seize the Day'*. Theo took Matthew's hand and gave it to him. He wanted Matthew to have it, he said. Matthew might be a bit young to hear all of the tracks, he whispered to me, as some contained a few swear words! Matthew was very chuffed with the CD. Theo then said a farewell to us. 'See you on the other side,' and with a smile he disappeared. We wondered what he had meant; the other side of what?

The three of us headed back for the tube station. Michaela was desperate to get home. We got on the tube to Euston. Michaela took a seat opposite us. As the train rattled around and gathered speed tears started to pour down her face. I leaned over and tried to tell her that her sheep would be kept safe. Something told me that this was a certainty. I do believe in a God and I do believe that God told me that Michaela's sheep would be saved. I told her that in the Bible there was a flock of sheep kept by Michaela. Maybe she thought that I'd lost it. I didn't care; it had to be said. A woman sitting next to us was looking on. I tried to explain to her what was happening back in Wales, and that Michaela feared for her sheep. The woman thought that it was a very bad situation. She had heard about what was going on in the country.

We reached Euston only to find there was no train for a while. We sat on the floor in the foyer and Michaela rang her husband. I suddenly decided not to go home but instead stay on for the night in London with Matthew. The NFU man's comments had unsettled me so much that I felt I could not return home without attempting to inform someone of what he had told us. Michaela ended her conversation with her husband and the news was that their sheep were still safe and sound. All the other farms had had their animals killed. I hated the thought of going back home. I asked Michaela what she thought of my idea of going to see someone at the press the next day. She agreed that the NFU man had said some fairly disturbing things and that it might be worthwhile to try to get someone to listen to what had happened. I started to write down what he'd said in a small notebook, and together we managed to remember all the important points.

The time came for Michaela to catch the train home. I started to be a bit panicky about what I'd decided to do. It wasn't as if I was on my own. Matthew was tired and we had no change of clothes or plan for where to spend the night. However, he said that he was content to stay on and so we bid farewell to Michaela. She seemed less troubled now and strode off briskly to catch her train.

Matthew and I went to see what the shops at the station sold, as we needed some things for the night. We found a Boots, where we bought toothbrushes and paste, soap and herbal sleep tablets; also some socks for us both. I did not like the thought of no change of clothes for the next day or any nightwear for us but here we were for the night, however stupid my idea.

When we came out of the station I rang Glyn to let him know that we were staying on for the night. He didn't know what to make of it all but tried to understand my reasons. I had a list of hotels in my guidebook and I rang one of them. The price for a room was too high so I tried another one that was located in a street called Ebury Street not far from Victoria Station. The price was reasonable and as time was getting on I booked a room for the night. I rang Glyn again to let him know the telephone number of the guest-house. I was becoming exasperated at the mobile, as it kept issuing a demand call to know our identity code, which I did not know. It had not done this before and made me quite uneasy so I switched it off and we headed off to catch a bus. As we left the station forecourt a young lad asked if we had any money to spare. I gave him a pound and happened to say why we were there. He said that what was happening to the farm animals was terrible. His grandfather was a farmer near Birmingham, he said, and feared for his livestock.

We caught a bus that would take us on a route through central areas of London. Evening was coming on and we needed to eat before going to the guest-house. I have no idea where we got off the bus but it was some fairly central road with restaurants and tourist shops. Around a corner we came to a pizza restaurant, which was a relief, as it was late and Matthew was getting fed up. We were glad of the rest and warmth and as we waited for the meal we talked a little about what had happened that day. Matthew was as shocked as I was about what the NFU man had said to us. It felt as if we had been thrown into some surreal time and place. Matthew told me that he thought there might be a plan to get rid of our farm animals in order to breed genetically modified ones. He also wondered if the rare breeds would be made even rarer and their genes kept in storage to sell for very high prices. My thoughts were much the same and I hope we will both be proved wrong.

It was dark when we left the restaurant. Matthew wanted to have a quick look in the little shop selling gifts for tourists. I was tormented with thoughts from the day and wished that we were really tourists with nothing but holidays on our mind. I bought a small resin paperweight for Matthew. It has a tiny model of Big Ben inside and whenever I look at it now I am always back in the little shop with all the weird miscellany of gifts for tourists, with its false sense of security from the darkness of the city street outside.

As we headed for a bus stop I told Matthew that I was going to phone the Telegraph office to find out if I could make an appointment to see someone the next day. A night shift reporter was there, who was very interested in what I told him of the meeting at the NFU. He said that I needed to speak with a man called David Brown and that I should ring the following morning. The way in which he seemed to take my concerns seriously made me feel less stupid for staying on for the night. We then went looking for the correct bus stop to take us to Victoria station. We found a stop, which we thought was the right one but after half an hour no buses had come past.

A woman walked by and told us that the route was not being used as road works nearby had made the buses temporarily take a different route. She said to follow her as she was going to wait at the same stop as the one we needed. The woman was very friendly and the conversation became centred on foot and mouth after she asked if we were on holiday there. She told us she was very fed up at what was happening in the countryside too, and could not understand what was going on. Over the two days that we were in London we met several folk of all nationalities who voiced a real concern for the plight of the animals, and this made me realise that it cannot be said that all city dwellers are indifferent to what happens in our countryside.

The bus for Victoria station arrived and we parted company with the friendly lady. We did not have to worry about knowing when we reached the stop for Victoria as the bus route ended there for the night. When we arrived at the station it had started to rain so we darted off to find Ebury Street and the guest-house. The rain became heavier and I didn't want to get the guide-book wet. I knew that we must be near to the street but in the darkness we could not make out which was the right direction. Two women in raincoats were walking towards us and I asked them the way. They told us that the street was very near but that we were walking in the wrong direction. They gave us details and walked on up the street. In a few minutes we saw the name Ebury Street on one of the corner walls. We walked on up the street and I stopped to check the book for the street number of the guest-house. Two women walked past us. I noticed their large earrings but did not think further than getting in out of the heavy rain.

We went to the door of the guest-house and rang the bell. By this time it was around 10.30 pm but there was a hall light on. Foot-steps thudded towards the door and a tall woman with auburn hair greeted us. She was very vague about my booking but asked us in. A man who I assumed to be her son swayed along the corridor towards us. He was drunk and the conversation between us was very muddled. The woman said that she did have a twin room and took us up to see it. Everything was quite depressing inside and the place did not sound at all like the one I had booked. No wonder because it turned out that we had the wrong guest-house; the one we wanted was next door.

The drunken son was becoming annoyed and wanted to know what was the problem. The woman told him off, then told me that she didn't mind which guest-house we stayed at. She said for me to go next door and see if there was anyone still up there. I went next door and rang that bell. A young smiling girl came to the door and said that yes we were expected and yes it was fine to come in. I went in and explained the mix up. The place was very welcoming and so I went back to tell the woman that we had decided to keep the original booking next door. I was really worried she would feel that we were messing her around but she was very good about it and gave me a card, saying that we could stay there at any time in the future if necessary. Her son came back into the hall and I just wanted to get out as fast as possible. The doorbell rang as I was picking up my bags. The man went to answer it and a hoard of yelling, laughing people came in with suitcases. We quickly escaped through them and hurried next door.

The room where we stayed was pleasant and quiet, down a corridor away from other rooms, but the night was filled with dread for me, and Matthew was a complete bundle of nerves too. I now know the reason for these feelings of apprehension, but that night there was just a sense of fear and neither of us knew why. The toilet was further on down the corridor and a wind had got up. There were two small open windows, too tough to close, along the corridor and when we had to go to the loo during the night the net curtains kept blowing in, brushing our faces. The windows looked out onto the back gardens and yards of the hotels along the street. All was black night except where it was punctured by a couple of lights still on. I had a ridiculous feeling of needing to keep out of sight whenever I had to pass by the windows and became very angry with myself. Matthew eventually went to sleep but I went over and over the day's events all night long.

Morning finally arrived and with it the need to sleep. However, there was something that had to be done that day and that was to try and speak with an interested concerned reporter. Poor Matthew was very tired too and we tottered along the corridor to go down for breakfast. The breakfast room was cheerful with walls covered in photographs of Wales. There were the Black Mountains, Talybont-on-Usk, views around the area of Abergavenny and there was Pen-y-Fan, the highest point of the Brecon Beacons. Marvellous panoramic views of Wales, the place of nightmares now.

The owner, Dafydd, came in to ask what we would like for breakfast. He is Welsh but has lived in London for several years. In between him bringing in the tea and scrambled egg we chatted and he told us that his parents had once been dairy farmers in South Wales. They had sold milk at the gate, he said, something that has now gone forever. I told him why we were in London and tried to explain what was happening back in Wales.

He was of the opinion that foot and mouth had to be eradicated as quickly as possible and was obviously not against what the Government was doing. I said how the animals were being killed when there was in fact no disease, but he did not seem convinced by my argument. I wonder what he thinks now.

After breakfast we went back upstairs to gather together our few things. We went to look out of one of the corridor windows. Everything looked so different in the morning light. There was row upon row of very ordinary back gardens stretching into the distance. It was raining again and in the small garden of the guest-house a bronze statue stood amongst the soaking foliage. The statue was of a woman, her head hung as if in tears. Her sadness mirrored my own.

10

Hannah

It was 4 April 2001. We said goodbye to Dafydd, then walked back to Victoria station to buy travel tickets for the day. The morning air was fresh from the rain and I was hoping that our stay would not be a wasted one. Window boxes and baskets full of spring flowers brightened the fronts of the plain hotels and guest-houses. I planned to go to the Daily Telegraph offices, then make an early start back for home. At the station I rang the number for David Brown. He said that he had some free time to see us that afternoon and I asked how to find the offices. The mobile started to play up and issued the demand call again, and then went dead. I didn't try again. After buying the tickets we decided to have a drink, as we both felt so tired, and we went into one of the station cafes. It was then that I began to have the feeling that we were being followed. I have never had the feeling before that day and have not had it since. At the time I put it down to the lack of a night's sleep.

We drank up and went off to get the tube to London Bridge. Ending up in Southwark instead we decided to get some lunch before going off to find the Telegraph offices. The traffic was very busy and as a bus came to a stop near us an elderly man with a white stick came to cross the road next to us. He smiled. I noticed what piercingly blue eyes he had. We crossed the road and went to have a quick look at Southwark Cathedral. There was restoration work going on so we did not stay. As we walked back from the cathedral to find a cafe the old man with the stick came by again.

Matthew and I had a baked potato in a small busy restaurant not far from the cathedral. Afterwards we set off in the direction of Tower Bridge. The day had brightened and we walked along by the Thames. Very soon though dark clouds were appearing; in the distance we could hear thunder.

We stopped at a shopping mall. I felt uneasy and wanted to turn back. The thunder became louder and the sky turned black. The high glass roof of the mall roared with rain and people ran inside for cover. I found a stall selling jewellery and bought a silver cross, covered in small silver flowers. We were not making much headway at reaching the office of David Brown.

The rain stopped and the sky cleared. Tower Bridge filled the view. I said to Matthew that we would not walk on any further. The day was speeding away from us, faster than the ferries going up and down the Thames, and I was beginning to wonder if we were going to find David Brown at all. We turned back and walked to catch a bus for the Telegraph offices. I asked someone which bus we needed. They gave us the wrong information so we wasted even more time. Eventually we caught a bus that took us to Moorgate, where I asked a man for directions to the Telegraph offices. He was puzzled and we then discovered that we had been given directions to the City offices and not the main office, which was in fact at Canary Wharf. If only I had rung David Brown back that morning. The man directed us to the City office of the newspaper. When we eventually stepped into the smart entrance hall we must have looked a bedraggled pair.

We were taken up to one of the floors of the offices, where we were met by a girl called Hannah. She was the office junior reporter and was exceptionally kind to us. She must have seen how tired we were. I explained that we had come down from Wales and had stayed over especially to speak with a reporter about what was happening in Wales with the foot and mouth. She made us a cup of tea and asked Matthew if he'd like to have a go on her computer. Then she rang the main office of the paper and spoke with someone in David Brown's office. He was at a meeting. Hannah handed me the phone. The man on the other end suggested that I write down what I wished Mr Brown to know. He was now unable to see us, which was understandable, as afternoon had turned into very late afternoon.

Hannah gave me some sheets of paper and I wrote sheet after sheet of what had been happening back home, and what had happened at the meeting at the NFU. On Hannah's computer there was a picture of a red fox leaping over an ice floe to safety. She gave Matthew details of how to download it and there was also a screen saver called 'Johnny Castaway' on a desert island. We still have him on our PC at home but the red fox disappeared one day and we never found out how to recover him. I keep meaning to contact Hannah. She was so wonderfully helpful. Nothing was too much trouble. She commuted from Kent each day and lived not far from where the early outbreaks of FMD had been. An Irish lady who worked there overheard our conversation. She asked me to write our contact details down because she knew some farming people who would be interested in contacting us.

I finished my writing. Hannah put the sheets into an envelope and placed it in the pigeon-hole for David Brown. She said that he was sure to have it by the next day and she thought that he would be bound to contact me. I never heard from him and it seems to me that the only positive thing to come out of that day was our meeting with Hannah, who inspired me to have hope and keep trying.

11

Rainbows and Flames

When we came out of the City offices afternoon was turning into evening, so we had to hurry to Euston for a train home, because otherwise it would mean another overnight stay. An hour or so later we were standing in the entrance of Euston looking at the information boards; not too long for our train. We went into WH Smith for a while and I bought a couple of books, one of which was '*Bird Song*', Sebastian Faulks' love story set in the First World War. It felt as if a war was going on in our country but that the casualties this time were animals. Matthew had a look through the game magazines and soon it was time to wait on the platform. We were very glad to see the train approach.

At last we were able to sit and rest. We sat next to two women who were travelling to Birmingham. Matthew tried to get the mobile to work. One of the women wondered if the sim card was not in place properly. It was. She didn't know what was causing it to keep making the demands for the retrieval number or why it was switching itself off. She thought it was very odd. Inevitably the conversation came round to FMD. The women minded a great deal about what was happening and were horrified to hear what had gone on at the NFU. They said that restrictions had been set up on the outskirts of Birmingham and they were very cynical about it all.

The sky was becoming ever more dark as evening wore on. As we approached the Midlands the sky was lit up by two rainbows so bright that all four of us watched them until they vanished. The train sped on nearer towards Birmingham and the sky took on an increasingly hostile hue, as if smoke was filling it from a distance. An evening sky was turning into the dread of home.

We found our train for Shrewsbury and at last felt able to have a rest. Then I saw a familiar face. Chris Musson, an archaeologist who had worked with Glyn at one time, was getting on the train. He sat in the next row of seats and I went to say hello. When I mentioned foot and mouth he said that he had driven down the road through Churchstoke that morning on his way from Aberystwyth to Shrewsbury station, and he had seen a huge pyre at the side of the road.

So it was true; they had burned the lovely creatures, the lambs and their mothers, the cows and their calves. I had somehow tried to make it not true, but now I knew that we would be going home back to the reality of what had been done to all those wonderful healthy creatures, many of them having just been born.

The train started up and soon Birmingham disappeared. City lights were replaced by blackness interspersed now and again by streaks of lights from towns and villages along the route. The mobile was still not working but each time the train did stop at a station we tried to contact Glyn. Each time the same demand came on for identity code and the phone went dead. We would have to contact him from Welshpool when we arrived.

A student was sat across the aisle from us. He had a large volume on Marx set out on the table. I could not help but ask him about it. He said that he was studying social history and psychology at Aberystwyth University. I asked about his views on Marx. He wasn't too sure what his views were. I told him about our trip to the NFU and how I believed there to be a very sinister plan to eradicate farming from Britain. He looked at me as if I was quite mad and said that I obviously needed a good sleep. His parents farmed in Cardiganshire and I do wonder if he has changed his opinions since our discussion that evening.

At one of the stations I jumped out to make the call to Glyn from the phone on the platform. Matthew was in a panic because he was afraid that the train would leave without me. But it was okay and I managed to let Glyn know that we were staying on until Welshpool instead of Shrewsbury. The remainder of the journey was spent mostly in silence and at around 9pm the train arrived in Welshpool. Glyn was there on the platform waiting for us and soon we were in the car coming back home. The familiar landscape now felt like some alien place where everything had changed. As we came over the brow of the hill above Churchstoke the darkness of the wide valley was lit up with flames from the pyres.

The sight of them made me want to flee the place. It was not home.

Tiredness had caught up but I had no peace that night. I took out the silver cross from its wrapping only to find that it had cracked on one side. That made me feel the evil all the more. Eventually we went to bed and slept an exhausted sleep.

The next day, 5 April, I went numb down one side of my body and had to get to the doctor. Glyn came home early from work and drove us to the surgery at Montgomery. I couldn't face travelling along the road where they had built the huge pyre so we took another road, through a village called Chirbury. All around us lay empty fields and plumes of smoke rose up amongst the trees and hedgerows along the way. I closed my eyes for much of the 6-mile journey and tried to shut it all out for a few minutes. The smell could not be shut out though, nor the anguish that had taken hold on our beautiful land.

The doctor diagnosed the numbness as stress related and told me that I must not try to do any more over the Foot and Mouth. The government could not be beaten, in his view, and he realised that all the culling was politically driven rather than any form of disease control. He told me that individuals could not beat this system and warned me that my health was in danger if I continued to fight on.

A week went by. I was lying in bed having my morning cup of tea, before getting up and it hit me. The two women who had walked past us on the night of 3 April in Ebury Street were the same women whom I had asked for directions. They had been walking away from Ebury Street so why had they passed a few minutes later along that very street? Why had they not told us they were walking that way? Then I thought of Theo and his environmental activities against the establishment. Had we somehow been associated with him when the cameras outside MAFF had been watching the people demonstrating there?

That night of 3 April my thoughts had been on finding the guest -house, and the women were of no consequence to me then. Suddenly I could picture them clearly as they walked slowly past us – their raincoats and their large earrings – most certainly the same women who had been walking the other way. When I got up I told Matthew and Glyn about the memory and my thoughts. Neither of them thought that I was being paranoid. Now I knew why I had such a feeling of being followed in London.

12

Four Crosses

The following Saturday, 7 April, our local newspaper carried a front-page story of a farmer whose animals were in danger of being drowned by floods and there was a plea for help. I managed to contact the farmer and offered any help we could give him. He told me there was very little that could be done and that he had reluctantly decided they would have to be destroyed. I told him that I was willing to help in obtaining a truck to ferry them to safety. He politely thanked me but told me that nothing could be done.

After the conversation I began to have misgivings about the farmer because he had seemed so adamant that the animals had to be destroyed and was not prepared to accept any help at all to save them. He lived some 50 miles away from where they were grazing and I could not understand why they could not be moved to higher ground or to his other holding. There were no restrictions in that area at the time, and therefore nothing to prevent the animals from being moved.

I rang the farmer back to tell him that we would try and obtain some help by the following day, Sunday. He sounded very odd for someone who had been offered help.

That afternoon and evening I rang through to various people on help lines but no hope of a lorry emerged. So the next day we set off to try and find the farm, which was situated near a village called Four Crosses. I bought an OS map from a garage and we went in search of what we assumed to be a farm near a flood plain in that area. After a couple of hours of searching for the place we stopped at a village service station. When I enquired, the lady told me to go and ask the man who was working in the shed nearby. The man was up to his elbows in engine oil but was very helpful. When I mentioned the name of the farmer he was quick to point out that the farmer in question was in fact a dealer. The farm we needed to find was called 'Rhandregynwen', the man at the garage told me, and this farm-land was not flooded. I thanked him for his help. He told me to be careful.

An April shower had changed to heavy rain as I left the garage. When I got back in the car I told Glyn and Matthew what the man had said. We had not been told the truth by the dealer and neither had the local paper. I now knew the directions for the farm and a few lanes later we were nearing a large, white, house with black windows. The sign at the gateway told us we had found the right place. We parked the car then I went to the front of the house and called out. There was no answer and the place seemed deserted. I could hear cattle shouting somewhere and I started to walk around to the back of the farm. At one side of the yard there was a long building with large dark arches along it. To the rear of the yard was a very large shed, and it was from inside this shed that the desperate sounds were coming from. There was an overpowering sense of evil and dread. I ran back to the car and asked Glyn to come around there.

There were several cars parked outside the shed. I felt too afraid to go nearer. Cowardice of seeing what they were doing to the cattle was the main reason. Glyn went off to the shed and I watched. Matthew came around to the yard and watched with me. We saw someone come to the shed door. The cattle stopped their terrible cries but started to bang on the shed walls. I was so afraid that they were going to be shot in there. Their fear was palpable and I said a prayer to myself.

Glyn walked back to us. The dealer had come to the door and had told Glyn that there was no choice but to have the animals destroyed. Glyn had managed to have a glimpse inside the shed as he spoke with the dealer. He had seen several people inside the shed crouched on the floor. The cattle had been bunched at the far end of the shed and Glyn had seen how terrified and panic-stricken they were. There was nothing that we could do. It was all so miserable there. Before we left I quickly took photos to prove that there was no risk of floods. In adjacent fields sheep and cattle were grazing contentedly but I wondered for how long.

As it happened, a long-standing friend of Glyn's, Paul Fowler, lives along a road near to that farm. He kept an eye out on the situation and told us that all was quiet for a few days but then Foot and Mouth posters began to appear along the road leading to the farm. A month later he saw RSPCA vans driving up and down from the place, then trucks of dead animals coming away from there. The animals belonging to the dealer were destroyed under the so-called welfare scheme. The RSPCA would have been well aware that the animals were perfectly well and not at risk from floods, but they still had condoned the action. I rang the RSPCA help-line about the matter, and was told, 'We are governed by MAFF'. This seemed such an astonishing statement that I thought I had misheard. I did write to the RSPCA head office to ask them about this and received a reply informing me that the RSPCA was definitely not governed by MAFF. However, their subsequent actions and attitude to the culling throughout 2001 caused me to believe the assistant on the phone.

13

Easter

13 April 2001, Friday, Good Friday. Our MP, Lembit Opik, was at the local Liberal Democrats office in Newtown and I made an appointment to see him. Matthew came with me. There is a stretch of road from Welshpool to Newtown that runs straight as a Roman road through a village called the Belan. Along this road there are several farms and the River Severn runs close by offering rich land for the grazing of the sheep and cattle and for the growing of crops.

As I drove along the road I looked at sheep contentedly grazing in fields near to the farm-houses, and the cattle in other fields, bright green from spring rain. It was so good to see them there, healthy and alive. Something bothered me about an army vehicle that was parked on the verge near to one farm. I drove on to Newtown.

Lembit Opik was in hectic mood. I told him how concerned I was about what was happening to the animals. He told me that he was in favour of vaccination and I said that I believed vaccination to be the right way forward also. The culling was inevitable though, in his opinion, because of the stance of the present government and he did not know how it could be stopped. I told him of my fear for the national flock and what had been said at the NFU. He appeared to take all the information on board and said that he would do what he could.

Afterwards Matthew and I went shopping in Woolworths for Easter eggs. I felt so despondent. The bright and shiny eggs in their boxes were unable to cheer me up and all I could think of was what was going to happen to the animals. They were at the mercy of a malevolent institution.

I drove back along the same road and as we neared the Belan we could see that the road had been blocked off. My heart sank. Army trucks were in view parked along the verges and I feared the worst. We made the necessary detour home. I rang some of the farmers in that area and the same old story unfolded. Cattle at one farm in the valley had been ill and all contiguous farms were to lose their livestock. Every farmer with whom I spoke, was resigned to the fact that their animals must go and I was so angry.

Over Easter weekend thousands of healthy sheep and cattle were killed in that beautiful valley. One farm after another lost their livestock to the devils. Mile after mile of farmland became desecrated and the poor animals were burned on a pyre that had been built up against a hedge bounding the main road. Holidaymakers on Easter Monday had to pass by the burning stench and the sight of the charred remains of cattle and sheep. Emotion erupted over that but it was too late for the animals. Compliance and money were getting the wicked job done.

Welshpool is a typical Welsh market town, with one of the largest livestock markets in Wales. I took Matthew shopping there a week or so after Easter. We could see the smoke from pyres on hills all around the town and the terrible stench filled the streets. The town was busy and maybe I was mistaken, but everyone seemed oblivious to the smell and to what was going on. How had they managed to shut it out? The streets stank of rotten barbecues and we were glad to leave the place. There seemed nowhere to hide though. Trucks that we recognised as the ones used to ferry the poor dead creatures kept passing by. Once, those trucks had been used for transporting animal feed stuff, but now they were the trucks of death, all neatly tied down with tarpaulin and looking so horribly innocuous.

Later the system perfected the transport even more and sealed trucks appeared on the roads. All the killing and suffering was hidden as much as possible from public awareness. Rendering plants took over from burial pits or pyres as a means of disposal in order not to offend the general public. How I hated the people who were at the heart of the wickedness. They hid behind a cloak of ineptitude or panic; neither applied. Mass murder was the truth of what was happening. I wanted to scream at people and tell them to wake up and realise what was happening to the beautiful creatures. Could they not see all the empty fields for mile after mile?

At Easter weekend I wrote to Professor Fred Brown, the world authority on FMD. I had managed to track him down at the beginning of April. It had taken hours to discover his contact number. Operators kept putting me through to anywhere but Plum Island. One number was a government department in Maryland and another a private address. The woman's name was Margaret O'Sullivan. Their flat looked out across the river to Cornell University and she wondered if Professor Brown worked there. It didn't sound the right place. Bird song drifted over her voice. Her husband was blind and he liked listening to the singing of his canaries, she told me. She was very angry about the killing of so many animals over here and wished me luck in finding Professor Brown. Everyone I spoke with had a word of encouragement to offer; they all found the mass culling of animals very wrong.

Eventually I was given the right department for Professor Brown and had been very surprised to hear a voice with a northern English accent on his answer phone. The next evening, the phone rang and it was Professor Brown. He told me that I had sounded desperate. I said that I was. The mass killing horrified Professor Brown too. He had grown up in an area near Manchester and he said how upsetting it was to hear of the killing going on in areas where he had once cycled as a young boy.

In my letter I asked him if he would be able to come over to try to persuade the Government to stop the killing and take alternative action. At the same time, unknown to myself, a woman called Alicia Eykyn had also contacted him to ask him to come over. She lives in Buckinghamshire and moves in circles of influence. Professor Brown faxed me back to tell me of her request and wrote that he was indeed coming over to the UK in an attempt to speak with the Prime Minister. The Prime Minister refused to meet him.

14

The Gelli Sheep

Eastertide passed and still the killing went on. Always the same story; cattle succumbing to sudden illness, then all surrounding farms taken out. One farm, near Builth Wells in South Powys, was deemed to be an infected premise, even though test results turned out to be negative. As a result, around sixty other farms were implicated and had their animals culled. The annual livestock show nearby was cancelled and movement restrictions set up for months, even though there had not been any disease whatsoever in the area.

On 22 April I heard that some elderly friends were being threatened with the loss of their small flock of sheep. Phoebe and Dennis have lived up at the Gelli for over 50 years and have always kept sheep. Their cottage sits high up in a hollow of a hill near Welshpool and when Matthew was a baby Phoebe helped lull him to sleep by pushing the pram across the fields. When Matthew was older we went to see their sheep and lambs, some kept cosy in their homely sheds. Phoebe and Dennis will not have sheep again and what they went through in April was unforgivable.

A so-called infected premise was declared at a farm in Buttington on 26 March. Several surrounding farms had their animals culled during the following fortnight but Phoebe and Dennis' sheep remained. A vet from the Ministry came to check on them in mid-April and said that they were fine. A few hours later, as Phoebe and Dennis sat in the Milk Bar in Welshpool, the vet telephoned again. She had made a mistake. Their sheep had to go. Dennis spoke with David Thomas, a senior Ministry vet and he confirmed that their sheep had to go. Dennis was very angry and Phoebe did not know where to turn. I rang them in the evening on 22 April and they said that they would fight it. I spoke with their son David, who farms not far from them. He did not know what to make of it all. He said that he had reinforced the fences and would help them try to keep the Ministry out.

On 27 April I had a reply from MAFF Animal Disease Control Division in London. I had written to request information on the policy in relation to FMD, and received a letter, enclosing several 'Public Information' fact sheets on 'Foot and Mouth Disease.' Fact sheet 3 was titled, 'What will happen if foot and mouth disease is suspected/confirmed.'

'If signs suggest FMD is present then the VO (Veterinary Officer), after consulting MAFF HQ, will sign a notice (Form C) which prohibits the movement of animals within a radius of 8 km of the premises concerned and arrange for sample material from the affected animals(s) to be sent to the Institute of Animal Health, by the quickest means possible.'

I read on. ' The VO reports the findings to MAFF HQ where the Chief Veterinary Officer will confirm the outbreak if the laboratory results confirm the presence of an FMD virus.'

But premises were being confirmed as infected premises even when results were returning as negative. In practice then, the stated policy of MAFF was not being followed.

The fact sheet went on to state, ' On confirmation of the disease an 'Infected Area' is imposed which extends to a minimum of 10 km around an infected premises,...' In Powys, and in other counties, 'Infected Areas' of 10 km were being declared around premises with negative test results, so again, policy was not being adhered to in practice. No sensible answer ever came back to my queries on these issues.

A week or so later I happened to be at the doctor's surgery in Montgomery. Dennis from 'Gelli' was sat in the waiting room. 'We still have the sheep' he told me. I was so glad that all was well. He looked pale and shaken. The Ministry had been there several times, he explained, and had even brought the police with a warrant. Phoebe came out from seeing the nurse. It was then my turn and afterwards we had a long chat about what was happening to them. Dennis was very cynical about it all and did not believe that their sheep should have to be killed. Phoebe was completely fed up and looked ashen. Dennis told me that he would fight them as much as he was able. They were afraid to leave the house though, they said, and feared that the Ministry would come to kill their sheep in their absence. Two ewes were due to lamb in the next few days. I told them that we would help in any way and we all left to go our separate ways back home.

Two weeks later I was told that they had lost their sheep. The person must have made a mistake, surely. No their sheep had been killed. A hollow feeling stuck inside me and would not leave. The prayers had not been answered after all. The lovely ewes and their lambs had been taken by the evil, and were incinerated in a mobile unit at Buttington, brought there following a failed burial of the sheep and cattle killed previously, whose poor bodies had risen to the surface of the burial site on the flood plain.

Almost two years went by before I spoke with Phoebe and Dennis again. We exchanged Christmas and Easter cards but it was not until February 2003 that I met them again. This time it was they who were offering a hand of help towards us in our trouble from DEFRA. The pain of what happened to their sheep still remains with them. Phoebe told us of how she kept having 'dreams of people in white suits coming to kill my sheep'. They seem lost without their sheep and Dennis has a quiet anger in him. Was it too much to ask that they be left alone to tend their flock of 27 sheep? Obviously so, because this couple who reared sheep for more than 50 years were forced to end those days with memories of the ewes and lambs 'slaughtered in the corner of the field at the back'. They were all healthy.

The killing continued as summer arrived. I began to be so incensed that I contacted newspaper after newspaper and eventually a reporter at the Sunday Times ran a piece on the fact that many so-called infected premises were not infected at all. There had to be a way of bringing the truth out.

A list of confirmed cases appeared on the MAFF website and also the Welsh Assembly website. I rang every farm listed for Powys. Not one of the farmers concerned was able to tell me that they had had positive test results for Foot and Mouth Disease. Many had been diagnosed clinically with no subsequent tests, several were still waiting for test results to be returned months after their animals had been slaughtered and some had been sent results when in fact no tests had ever been conducted on their animals.

I rang various Animal Health Department help lines frequently and sometimes managed to glean information out of some of the folk at the other end. One conversation that I recall clearly was with a lady vet on the Ministry help line. I asked about the testing procedure and why it was taking so long in some cases. She told me that they had to wait for anti-body results and if the result was negative they had to wait longer to make sure that it was negative. I explained to her that having spoken with dozens of farmers in Powys it was becoming plain that farms were being falsely diagnosed, but even if test results were later known to be negative the farms were still listed as infected premises. She had no answer or explanation. One day I rang on behalf of a farmer and was given the information that the test result of that particular farm was negative so far, but that they had to wait for a definite negative result. Again, I asked why the farm was being listed as an infected premise and all surrounding farms taken out. Again, there was no explanation. I was appalled at the attitude of the vets; they must have known that they were engaged in disingenuous work and yet they carried on. Was there anyone who was not willing to be bought by this destructive system?

15

Mrs Jones

On 14 May I happened to have a conversation with a lady in South Powys. She was a Mrs Jones and I chose her number at random from the farmers section of the Yellow Pages just to see how things were in that area, which was not far from Brecon. Since that time I have not been able to find her number again but her influence proved mighty.

We talked for over an hour. She was a widow and had brought up her disabled son who had been left mentally disabled after an accident. Her view of the Ministry was highly cynical and she told me of a visit made a few years back by a MAFF official. Even then she had been aware that they wanted to get rid of small farms and she had openly asked the official. His reply had confirmed her fears. During our conversation she told me of how she had taken her disabled son to America for treatment. I shall always remember her words in relation to her commitment towards her son. 'You can achieve anything if you are determined enough'.

The next day, 15 May, I was having breakfast when the phone rang. It was Mrs Jones and she had news of a farmer who had barricaded their farm driveway against the Ministry. She did not know the name of the farmer but only that they lived about ten miles away and that the farm was near Bronllys, which is a village near Talgarth in South Powys. I started ringing around any farmer who I could find as listed in that area. After 30 minutes or so I found a farmer who knew that the farmers were the Lloyds of Pentre Sollars. He gave me their number and I rang immediately. The phone rang for quite some time and I had nearly given up hope when a voice answered. It was Mrs Lloyd, or Eleanor as I now think of her. She sounded quiet and very distraught. I quickly explained why I was ringing and told her that they did not have to agree to give up their animals. Her tone changed. She sounded overjoyed. 'Oh thank you. I shall go and tell them now. The army is outside the gate, and the vets, and police and there are trucks waiting by the road to take our animals. We were about to give in but I shall go and tell them now. '

Later on that afternoon Eleanor rang back. Everyone had backed off and gone away after a long while of dispute. She was so relieved as was her son Robert and husband Winston. She told me that several people had arrived outside their gate to demonstrate against the proposed cull. This was the result of a message for help that I had put on the internet that morning. BBC Wales also turned up and the Lloyd's stand against the cull spread across Wales.

Eleanor said that they were very worried though that the officials would return and force them to comply. The Ministry vet seemed to be on their side, she felt. He had been a vet during the outbreak of 1967. I had spoken with him earlier that afternoon and he had been very angry that I had been given his mobile number. I had asked him to help prevent the Lloyds from losing their animals, as they were healthy and they wanted to keep them. He became a little less angry but told me abruptly that I must get off the phone and let him get on with his job. During a phone conversation with Eleanor many months later, she said that she had heard the vet ask a policeman at the gate if he had heard of someone called Janet Hughes. The policeman had. The vet apparently said that 'she's a bloody nuisance.' However, he made sure that the Lloyds kept their animals. He tested them frequently and all results returned negative. The Lloyds took legal advice and MAFF eventually gave in altogether. Pentre Sollars Farm was the only one out of forty in the area to keep their livestock.

One day I hope that I shall trace Mrs Jones and thank her for saving the day. Eleanor has tried to think who she might be but there are so many farmers who have the name of Jones that it is very difficult to track her down. If she had not telephoned me that morning it is highly probable that the Lloyds would no longer have their closed flock of traditional Welsh sheep or their dairy herd.

That same week there was a television news bulletin on BBC Wales, which said that the Welsh Assembly was allowing sheep to be moved back onto common land of the Brecon Beacons. This was good news, on the surface, but there was something very worrying about it. Why, with all the restrictions still in place in Wales, was the Assembly agreeing for thousands of sheep to be moved onto the Brecon Beacons? The sheep had been wintered on the lowlands of Pembrokeshire and were being moved many miles. Something about this gave me great fear.

16

The FMD Truth Rally

On 3 June we held a rally in Llandrindod Wells, where the main Animal Health offices for Powys were situated. A couple of weeks earlier I had been having a chat with a dairy farmer in Worcestershire, Nicola Morris, and the idea was formed. There would be several rallies at places wherever someone could organise one. Nicola planned one for outside the MAFF offices in Worcester, a lady up in Cumbria organised one for Penrith and some farmers in Cornwall also organised one.

Each rally had a large banner with 'FMD TRUTH RALLY' printed boldly in white on black. We cut two large hazel branches from the tree in our garden, which we used as poles to hold the banner high. The rally was held on Sunday 3 June. We were up early and I was very nervous because I had never organised anything like this before and I was also very worried that nobody would come along. Messages had been put on the internet and various Welsh papers had carried the story but I was still very apprehensive.

The morning was lovely and sunny; a real summer's day. We loaded up the car with the banner and poles, and the various leaflets for distribution. There was also a sheet of questions to give to the person in charge at the Animal Health Office.

As we drove into Llandrindod Wells we saw a large group of white doves fluttering and strutting on the pavement. I hoped that it was somehow a good sign. We were early as we drove through the main entrance to the offices. There is a large lake at the front and as we drove round to find a car park we saw a woman standing as if on patrol. She was wearing an identity card. I asked Glyn to stop the car and I went to ask her where we needed to park, as we had come to a rally. She pointed out the direction and we parked. There were a few people in the car park already and some of them looked as if they might be farmers.

A car pulled up and a tall fellow climbed out. He had a long cut on his face and bruises. It turned out that he was the Special Branch policeman from Brecon, and he had had a tough game of rugby on the Saturday. We shook hands and he introduced himself. We had spoken on the phone the previous afternoon, when he had phoned after reading the news reports of the proposed rally. I think he realised that we were very ordinary people and not extremists who were going to cause trouble. The other policeman drew me aside and went over why they were there; just to make sure all went smoothly. It all seems so ironic now because I was so shy and nervous and yet here were Special Branch people checking on us, as if someone feared a riot.

Arwyn and Elaine, who we had met at the Royal Oak back in April, turned up and we had a quick chat. Then a tall man came up and introduced himself as Mr John Pugh. He is a farmer near Rhayader in Powys. We had had several heated telephone conversations over the weeks and here he was at last, looking fairly jovial. He introduced a farmer friend, Mr Gatehouse. Then Mr Pratt arrived on the scene. He immediately grabbed my sheet of questions and shouted for everyone to listen. By now quite a good crowd had gathered. The camera-man from HTV was there too. The crowd grew silent. Mr Pratt started to read out the questions, but then began to question my motives for organising the rally. I said that I believed, like many other people, that there should be a public inquiry into the handling of Foot and Mouth. He seemed determined to argue with me and I was equally determined to stand up for myself.

The cameraman was capturing the debate and I do wonder if the film is still in existence somewhere in their archives. Mr Pratt boomed on, and more and more people started to voice their opinion. A lady who owns a cafe near Brecon was supportive of the rally. In her view the culling was totally unnecessary and very cruel. She supported the stand for a public inquiry. I could not understand Mr Pratt's determined effort to undermine the rally. He farms beef cattle and had been very against the proposed cull at the Lloyds, Pentre Sollars, so why was he set against me? The answer lies in the fact that I am not a farmer. I tried to explain to him that I come from a farming family and that I grew up on a smallholding with sheep but he did not want to listen.

The policeman mercifully called to me that it was time for us to go over to County Hall. The crowd moved away from Mr Pratt and I retrieved my file of questions from his grasp. His attitude had made me angry and I forgot to be nervous. Glyn, Matthew and I walked in front with the banner held high. Slowly we crossed the road and headed for the offices. Phil, the HTV man, walked ahead, filming as we went. We walked over the disinfected straw and Phil said that he knew which entrance we needed. The road curved round the building and we followed him to the main door. There was no answer and the building seemed deserted. Had I made a dreadful error in organising the rally for a Sunday? Mr Pratt would make a meal of me if I had.

We called to the crowd behind that we had to turn around because nobody seemed to be answering the door. The banner was becoming heavy and awkward. Suddenly a window opened and a woman leaned out. She told us that there was nobody from Animal Health working there. I could hear angry mutterings from the supporters. They seemed to be angry with the woman though, as they did not believe her. Phil was very suspicious too and he led us back round to the front of the offices. It was then that someone spotted cars parked in a car park adjacent to where we had parked. There was a smaller building behind some trees and sure enough as we got nearer we could see a sign for a meeting there. So this was where the officials were hiding.

Phil took the lead again and we marched up to the entrance. I went to ring the bell. A man came to the door. What did we want? I gave him the list of questions. The man was Gary Haggerty, an official of the Welsh Assembly Animal Health Division. He read the sheet, which included questions such as how many farms were in fact infected with FMD, and how many animals had been culled unnecessarily. I explained that people wanted the truth, hence the reason for our rally. The official said that he would make sure that the questions were answered in due course and we left. No reply was ever provided by the Welsh Assembly or the Ministry.

I had a sheet for people to sign if they believed that there should be a public inquiry, so quickly I rushed round to ask, as some people were starting to leave. People stopped leaving and little clusters of discussion began to form. I took the sheet up to a group of four men, one of whom was Mr Pratt. He told me that he was telling people not to sign it. Now I was really angry and I let him know it. He boomed at me in the loudest voice that I have ever encountered. I was simply not the right type of person to be doing this. I was not a farmer. He obviously resented my presence very much and I resented his biased opinion against me. In the end we chose to disagree and the booming subsided. The three farmers next to him signed the petition and did not seem to have a problem with my not being a farmer. They could see that I cared about what was happening to farming.

Quite a few people signed the form but some did not wish to do so, and I wondered how many of them had been influenced by Mr Pratt's comments. Phil from HTV had left to go to a wedding and most of the supporters were leaving. We stayed there for a while, talking with the farming couple, Arwyn and Elaine, and a woman from Llandegley, near Llandrindod Wells, who had been voicing her opinion against the culls in the local papers. After 30 minutes or so the door to the smaller building, where the meeting had been held, opened and several people filed out to their cars. We wondered what the meeting had been about. The car-park emptied and we left too.

The banner was rolled up and the long hazel poles tied back on the roof rack ready for the return home. We said goodbye to Arwyn and Elaine, who seemed to think that the rally had gone well. As we drove back out of the main entrance I saw a statue on the verge. It was a figure of a woman cradling a lamb. Glyn stopped the car and I went to have a closer look. The figure was entitled 'Gaia'. I took a photo. It seemed as if irony was heaped upon irony for such a symbol of peace and creation to be standing outside the very place where plans were being made for the destruction of the wonderful creatures.

17

Election Day Dragon

7 June, Election Day, dawned. Tony Blair was driving a knife into the heart of our countryside and yet it seemed inevitable that he would return to power. Matthew came with me to Welshpool and I voted at the school there. In the yard there was skip piled high with stuff that they were throwing out. Right on the top was perched an enormous papier-mache dragon, painted Welsh red and breathing flames of shiny paper. He was absolutely wonderful and he came home with us. One of the teachers was very pleased that he was being given a new home. The day that we found him seems to mark a point in time when the fight to save the animals intensified.

When we had arrived back late in the afternoon I had made a cup of tea and was musing over an odd map that I had found by a bin at the entrance to Powis Castle, a National Trust property near Welshpool. All the animals from that estate had been culled at Easter. Welsh black cattle of rare blood-lines had been lost and all the sheep from the various farms which make up the estate. The map, which was a torn half-page from a computer generated map, showed main routes in North Wales and the Midlands, and also reservoirs, lakes and rivers. Some major roads looked to be more important than other major roads because they were highlighted in strange black track lines. Route lines leading to Bangor and Skipton and coastal areas were highlighted and routes leading to ports such as Liverpool. There were numbered places and number 2 was named 'Untitled Bangor.' Unfortunately the map was torn off just above Welshpool and therefore I have never been able to find out if Powis Castle had relevance or not. Number 1 was in the West Midlands.

The phone rang and it was Chris Stockdale, an organic farmer from Herefordshire who had lost many of his cattle and sheep in the spring to a cull. He told me that he had been speaking with a woman who lived near

Hay-on-Wye in South Powys. The woman had been in a pub the night before and had overheard a conversation between some slaughter-men. She had given Chris the telephone number of one of them and he was ringing to ask me if I would contact him. I did not like the idea at all. The thought of a slaughter-man is enough for me and I did not want to speak with one. Nevertheless I said that I would phone the man to see what information, if any, he was willing to give.

I phoned him around tea-time as Chris had mentioned that the man usually went out for a drink in the evening. The man answered the phone. I took a silent deep breath and told him the reason for my call. He sounded wily. However, he gave a great deal of information, much more than I could ever have imagined. He said that as long as his name was not mentioned to anyone he did not mind me using the information. Matthew had come into the room. He handed me a piece of paper and a pen. The man asked me if I was writing down what he was saying. I told him that I was not, which was not strictly true.

As he began to tell me what he knew it all became more and more alarming. He told me that there had been a meeting held by officials on 3 June. The man would not say where it had been held but it was about 'orders from the MAFF.'

'There are lorries,' he continued, 'on standby in various secret locations. Eighteen slaughter-men are booked into the Metropole in Llandrindod Wells and the army too, and in a hotel in Brecon'.

'The idea', he said 'is to clear all Powys, from Monmouth to Rhayader, the Elan Valley, Epynt, Black Mountains, Brecon Beacons. All Powys. They'll find something even if it's Orf.' (Orf is a contagious disease of sheep, which causes blisters in and around the mouth.)

He said that they had been told that they would be 'flat out' in July and had been told not to book any holidays. His words were so horrifying and I could tell that he was telling the truth. He also mentioned a site for burning/burial that 'is already earmarked, and has been cleared.' I asked if it was the site near Kerry and he said 'It might be. It has been in the paper'. A few weeks earlier there had been uproar in the village of Kerry, which is 10 miles from where we live, because plans had been discovered for a burn site high on the Kerry Ridgeway.

The man had more to say. He told me that the National Parks were involved. That gave meaning to the many outbreaks that seemed to keep falling on the edges of National Parks across Britain. I asked if he thought it possible that more culling would go on in Montgomeryshire and he said 'There's not much left there, but we might be back round your way'. Our conversation then ended and I thanked him for telling me what he had. He told me that he would let me know if he heard anything else and I was very surprised by this. I did wonder if he was just saying this in order to have my contact details but he kept his word and several weeks later gave me more information.

When I came off the phone I started to shake uncontrollably. I had tried very hard whilst speaking with the man to remain calm and objective, because I felt he would give more information then. However, now the full impact of his words hit me. Glyn had come home and I told him of the conversation. This man was part of the plan, part of the killing machine, but he was willing to give out information. He was an old-fashioned slaughter-man, the type who went round to individual farms, and had a 'cup of tea and a piece of cake', as he'd mentioned. Even he found the current actions offensive and he knew that there was a plan to end sheep farming in Wales. He was no longer part of a more normal farming cycle of life and death; only a system of death and he did not care for it.

I made a proper copy of the quick notes that I had made during the conversation and faxed them to the local reporters. The only reporter ever to get back about it was Sue Goddard, a reporter with the Western Mail. She left to live in Scotland in the autumn of 2001 and I miss her determination to get at the truth. In late spring she had written a report on a poster that had been printed for Foot and Mouth. I had happened to stop and read one of them in detail and had noticed that the date of printing them by Powys County Council had been 21 February 2001. The posters stated 'Infected Area' and applied to Powys. It had struck me how odd it was that they should have been printed only two days after the initial outbreak in Essex had been reported on 19 February and in fact several days before any outbreak was reported in Wales. The movement ban had only been brought in on 23 February but already Powys County Council had been busy preparing these posters for infected areas. It seemed too efficient for my liking. Sue Goddard spoke with a man from Trading Standards and I did also. He was full of excuses but said that 'in hindsight it was a mistake to have printed the date'.

Sue believed my information on the slaughter-man and she spoke with him on the phone. He gave her his name and confirmed what he had told me, but would not let her divulge his identity. She was therefore unable to report it. If only he had felt braver.

In the evening I put out information about the map that I had found near Powis Castle on the Sheepdrove chat site and asked for any information on transporting dead animals from docks. The next day, 8 June, I received a phone call from someone who called himself 'Charlie'. He told me that he worked at the docks in Hull; King George V docks. In a shaky voice he said that they were transporting dead animals from that dock. They were being put into huge metal skips weighed down with concrete bars. He sounded so wound up and genuine. I believed him, even though subsequently several people ridiculed me and eventually shut me off the chat site. However, I have tape recordings of telephone conversations with various officials at the docks and one woman, in particular bears out Charlie's story. She was the telephonist at Associated British Ports in Hull and I explained to her that I had been informed that truck-loads of dead animals were being transported out to sea from the docks in metal containers. I asked her if it were true. She hesitated, but then said, 'Well...well... we do..do them through the docks'. Then she transferred me through to the Operations Manager, who of course, went on to totally refute this, but the telephonist's comments remain on my tape.

8 June also brought the news that Blair was back in power. My heart sank.

Not long after the elections MAFF became DEFRA, Department of the Environment, Food and Rural Affairs. Agriculture no longer had a mention.

On 16 June I received a letter from Dr Alex Donaldson, Head of Laboratory at the Institute of Animal Health, (IAH), in Pirbright, Surrey. I had written to him asking for his opinion of the mass culls and of DEFRA's failure to follow standard procedures in relation to testing. His reply was fairly dismissive really and he attempted to support DEFRA's scientific policy of testing, based on a 95% confidence of detecting a 5% prevalence of antibody. I subsequently fowarded his letter on to Professor Brown, who wrote back to say that this made no sense to him, and that he wondered if Alex Donaldson understood it either. Dr Donaldson also wrote that he doubted that animals known to have antibodies were spared in the 1967-68 epidemic. So I sent him photocopies of the relevant pages from the Northumberland Report 1968, which cited the examples of sheep with antibodies not being a danger and not being culled.

The ironical part was that whilst in his letter he stated that carrier sheep were a potential danger to other animals, he had enclosed a copy of a chapter from a book that he had written jointly with other scientists. It was entitled Diseases of Sheep, and one paragraph confirmed that carrier sheep had never been shown to infect other animals in experimental conditions. So, the Dr Donaldson writing to me as Head of Laboratory at the IAH seemed to be at odds with the Dr Donaldson, the independent, impartial veterinary scientist.

By this time I was in contact with several people in Cumbria, including Moira Linaker and Suzanne Greenhill. I had read of the fight by Moira Linaker to save her flock of Ryeland sheep from the cull, and had managed to contact her in late spring. The same system of mass killing in the absence of test results appeared to be the order of the day in Cumbria too. Moira was determined that her flock would stay alive and she succeeded in defending them from the slaughter.

Will Cockbain, the then NFU chairman in that area, had put me in contact with Suzanne after I had spoken with him about the meeting at the NFU back in April. Will had been very interested indeed, and very concerned, to learn what we had been told by the senior official of the NFU.

Suzanne, whose ancestors had founded the large auction mart in Cockermouth, was highly sceptical of the culling policy and we had many frustrated conversations over the phone, exchanging information about what was happening in our particular areas. It was heartbreaking to hear about the mass slaughter of the Herdwicks and Swaledales, breeds that are now in serious decline. The 'voluntary' cull in Cumbria had been voluntary in word only; it was the same compulsory pre-emptive culling that was happening in Wales and other areas of Britain, including Devon and Yorkshire. Farmers who refused to allow their flocks to be culled in the scheme were placed under great pressure to conform to the rules and as a result few fought against the cull. Many of them agreed to the cull of their sheep to save their dairy cattle, only to lose their cattle to the slaughter if one sheep was found to be sero-positive. To me it seemed like one demonic killing spree.

18

Fears of Mass Cull

On Monday 18 June, a public meeting was held by NFU Cymru, at the Royal Welsh Show-ground at Builth Wells. We set off as soon as Glyn came home from work. Jill Byron, a woman who kept horses up near the Longmynd in Shropshire, and who we had met through local newspaper letters, came with us. She has a great anger also about the government's attitude to farming and a great frustration that nothing seems to stop them in their onslaught against the farming community.

The meeting had been called in order to allay fears that had been circulating about a mass cull in Powys; all rumour according to officialdom, as reported in various newspapers. When we arrived at the show ground there were several land rovers and cars turning in there and the place looked busy. We parked the car then walked down to the main building. Frank Lockyer and Rob Shelley from HTV were outside the entrance. Frank is a cameraman for HTV and Rob is the reporter for Mid-Wales. I had met Frank when they came to film about the Truth Rally and he makes one feel very at ease in front of the camera. We had a short chat and went into the hall. It was very crowded. We found some seats near the back and I looked around to see if anyone I knew was there. No one yet.

More and more people poured into the large room and soon all seats were full. Time for the start of the meeting arrived. People still kept coming in and soon many were left with standing room only. At the front there was a row of seats for the officials and we now saw Tony Edwards, the Chief Vet for Wales, taking his place. To my mind he looked uneasy. The room quietened. A man stood up to announce the start of the meeting and to introduce the officials. Sitting next to Tony Edwards was Gareth Jones, Director of FMD Operations for the Welsh Assembly. He was apparently attending instead of Carwyn Jones, the Rural Affairs Minister, and we could hear muffled waves of anger amongst the audience that Mr Jones had refused to attend as requested. Huw Richards of NFU Cymru was there, looking quite rosy cheeked and as if he was at an agricultural show.

The meeting got underway. Mr Jones began by saying that there was no truth to the rumour of a mass cull in Powys. The room rippled with voices of disbelief. Mr Edwards looked very uneasy. After the posturing came the questions from the audience. Farmers wanted to be told the truth and one by one they stood up to ask questions. What was happening with regards to all the restrictions on movement? Why were farms being culled out when they were not infected, and how long were they to going to have to put up with all this?

The questions kept coming and the officials kept weaving in between them. I wanted to ask a question about antibodies. Edwin Roderick, a farmer from the Epynt area, took the microphone. The Epynt is a mountainous region owned mostly by the Ministry of Defence and it was there that a mass burn site had been sited. There had been uproar and in the end Carwyn Jones had relented and the burning had ceased. In the interim however many thousands of healthy animals had been sacrificed, many burnt alive in the vast pit and the water-courses polluted from the poor animals' fluids. Edwin Roderick wanted answers but he was given platitudes. He sat down, looking very dissatisfied.

I kept my hand up and eventually the microphone was passed to me. My question was to Tony Edwards. I asked him why were whole flocks being slaughtered on the basis of one animal testing positive for anti-bodies. Mr Edwards stuttered and admitted he was unable to answer the question. He looked very awkward and passed the question over to Ruth Watkins, a retired virologist who keeps sheep in Carmarthenshire and who has grazing rights on the Brecon Beacons. She verified that there is no evidence to show that an animal that tests positive for a FMD antibody is able to infect other animals. Matthew stood up to point out that in the 1967 FMD outbreak animals with antibodies were not killed. I was very proud of him.

Gareth Jones and Tony Edwards began to look less sure of themselves than they did at the start of the meeting. Farmers jeered Mr Jones when he tried to tell them that no healthy animals had been killed in the preceding weeks. Mr Edwards looked increasingly uncomfortable and as if he was fed up with the onerous duty of telling lies.

A man stood up at the front and was given the microphone. He told everyone that he was a vet and had worked for MAFF for a very short time, (just one day as he later told us). He had stopped working for them because he believed that they were not acting within the law and he had been present when a dreadful cull of healthy animals had occurred at Knowstone in Devon. He told the farmers that they had rights and could refuse to allow their animals to be culled.

After about two hours Huw Richards, the NFU Cymru official, thanked Mr Edwards and Mr Jones for turning up. The organiser of the meeting also thanked them, and then the meeting ended. Mr Edwards' expression changed to one of relief and he left his seat very quickly. Several people went to the front in order to ask the officials more questions, and both Mr Jones and Mr Edwards disappeared amongst a sea of inquiries.

We went to speak with the vet, whose name was Julian Heath and we exchanged contact details. He is a man of great Christian belief and had faith that the present evil would be overcome but only if the farmers woke up and started to fight against MAFF's actions. After a quick chat with Arwyn and Elaine, and Michaela, we left and drove back through the disinfectant and on into the dark of the night and the long journey home. None of us knew what to make of the meeting, but all of us felt that there was a conspiracy at the heart of it all and fears of a mass cull still remained. Midnight saw us arriving back home. Jill collected her car and after waving her off we went straight to bed.

I felt angry at myself for not standing up and telling everyone at the meeting about the slaughter-man's information. The problem was that I had no hard evidence to back it up, but I still felt like kicking myself for not speaking out.

19

One for Sorrow

The next day, Tuesday 19 June, was a fairly humdrum day until late evening. At around 10.40 pm the phone rang. It was Nick Green from Cumbria, a man who was totally against the culling policy and who had been protesting against the ministry's actions. His voice sounded very shaky and distressed. He told me that a horrific cull of cattle was happening at that moment near Skipton in Yorkshire. Apparently, the owner was absent. Nick was in a very distraught state and I felt completely helpless. It was pitch dark and I could not quite believe that MAFF was hounding animals at that time of night. But of course, they were. I told Nick that I would try to help, although I hadn't a clue how. He rang off.

I decided to phone the Skipton police station. The officer who picked up the phone knew immediately what I was talking about. His attitude was distressing in itself. He told me in a very matter of fact way that if it was to do with FMD, then it was 'up to the MAFF'. So, it was acceptable for animals to be killed in a most dreadful way at any time of day or night. It was **not** acceptable.

Another officer came to the phone. He told me that they had no jurisdiction at all and said that he would put the phone down on me. In the end I did. It was all so wicked. Where would it all end, I wondered. Would there be any farm animals left?

On Wednesday 20 June Matthew and I were returning home through the village of Llandyssil near Montgomery. It was a lovely summer afternoon. As we turned a corner we could see a young crow ahead sat right in the middle of the narrow road. I stopped the car and the truck behind us overtook. The young crow made no move to escape when I went to pick it up. He was not visibly injured and his dark eyes were bright in the sun. We took him to one of the fields and placed him carefully in the grass hoping that his parents would find him. He seemed very forlorn and sat there amongst the summer grass making no move at all. Matthew and I returned to the car and sat in a small lay-by for a while. Then we walked back to the field. The young crow had not moved and there was no sign of other crows about. I was worried that he would starve if left on his own because he seemed too young to be able to fend for himself. So, maybe in error, I decided to pick him up and bring him home.

He sat on Matthew's lap in the car and looked very content. When we arrived home we took him upstairs out of the reach of our cats, and he stayed in Matthew's bedroom for the night. We offered him all sorts of food that we thought might be appropriate but he was not interested. He did like being held and eyed us intently as he sat in our laps as if in a forgotten nest. We went to bed worrying that we may have done the wrong thing by bringing him home and decided to return him to the field the next morning.

21 June, Mid Summer's day, a beautiful morning; clear blue skies and the hope of a good day ahead. The crow seemed quite bright thankfully, but still did not want to eat anything. I stroked his shiny back of blue black feathers and he looked at me in a sad way. In a few minutes we were going to take him back to his fields. I went out to pick some grass for him before we left. When I went back upstairs to him a couple of minutes later he was dying. I picked him up gently and placed the fresh grass next to him. It was so terribly sad. Outside the morning sun was gleaming and the poor crow was leaving it all, with no hope of returning to his fields. I cried and felt that I had failed. One moment he had seemed fine and the next he had gone. Mid Summer's day lost its brightness and took on a foreboding nature.

20

Libanus

On the afternoon of Saturday 23 June Mr Gatehouse, from Llangorse, telephoned. There had been an outbreak of foot and mouth, he said, at a farm near the village of Libanus, which lies at the foot of the Brecon Beacons. He felt sure that something had happened the night of the meeting on 18 June. I felt a great dread. Was this the start of the mass cull?

Mr Gatehouse told me the names of the farmers concerned. The first farmer I spoke with was Edwin Harris, Chairman of the Graziers' Association. He had several farms and had apparently been informed by DEFRA that all his animals would probably have to be culled as dangerous contacts. The thing that bothered me greatly was that he sounded completely resigned to the fact. There was no hint of a wish to fight in his voice, which made me angry. As Chairman of the Graziers' Association he had a huge influence and the graziers would follow his lead I felt. However, if he had given up I had not.

I asked him for some names and numbers and he told me of some of the farmers threatened with loss of their livestock. The next farmer I spoke with was Mrs Phillips whose husband Tom was Secretary of the Brecon Beacons Commoners' Association. They were going to fight it, she told me in her gentle but determined voice. I spoke with Mr Phillips, and he sounded determined too. That was Saturday. By Sunday his voice had a totally different tone. He was going to try to fight them on this, he told me, but he sounded like a man who had given up hope. What had happened since the previous day? He knew that his stock was healthy but he was at the mercy of the same conniving trick as I had heard before; your livestock must go to safeguard your neighbour's.

By Monday 25 June all animals on farms contiguous to Modrydd Farm had been killed; thousands of healthy sheep and cattle wiped out for mile after mile along the valley, before any test results had been known. Mr Phillips had given in and his animals were gone when I next spoke with him. He sounded a broken man but told me that he had let his flock in the valley go in order to save the large flock up on the common land of the Beacons. It was heart-rending to hear the quiet distress in his voice. He told me how the vet, a Mr Sinclair, had wanted to monitor the sheep, but when Mr Sinclair had phoned the State Veterinary Service in Cardiff, his decision had been overruled and it was ordered that they be killed.

On 26 June there was a news report that sheep were being gathered from the lower slopes of the Brecon Beacons to be tested. What the report did not mention was that these sheep were being killed at the same time. All went quiet for the next few days.

21

Wolverhampton

On Sunday 1 July we went to Wolverhampton to a meeting organised by the National Foot and Mouth Group, a group that had its origins in the internet chat group on the Sheepdrove web-site. Initially I had planned to take a train but Michaela rang to offer us a lift. Phil Owens, the FUW local representative, was coming too and when Michaela picked us up she was flustered because she was late. Phil would be annoyed she feared. I felt lucky to have a lift at all. Phil Owens was waiting in Forden and jumped out of his car. His wife was there too. She told us of a group of foreign people who had come through the village in a bus the other day. Apparently they had been looking for work connected with culling. It all sounded so strange. What on earth was going on?

The meeting was held at the Britannia Hotel near to the Grand Theatre, where we had taken Matthew to see pantomimes in the past. By the time we arrived, the foyer was already filled with groups of people and from what you could hear from their conversations, they seemed to have all come for the meeting. Arwyn and Elaine were there and we sat down by them. A news reporter for 'Midlands Today' came in to ask if there were any farmers who would wish to be interviewed. There were not many farmers there; only Arwyn and Elaine it seemed and Christopher Stockdale, the farmer from Herefordshire. When we had gone into the foyer I had recognised his voice and we had a brief chat. Arwyn went out to speak with the reporter. A few moments later the reporter returned and asked me if I'd like to say something too. Something he said keeps coming back to me. He told me that even if you only have the chance of a minute or so on TV to get information out it is important to grab that time at every opportunity. Whenever I see him reading the news on Midlands Today I think of what he said.

We were called in for the start of the meeting. Tony, who was a pig breeder from near Welshpool, had elected himself as Chairman. He stood up and grandly opened the meeting. Then a man sitting at the front stood up and declared that Tony should not have elected himself as Chairman. The man declared that he wanted to stand as Chairman anyway. The TV crew left at this point.

Tony was eventually voted as Chairman and the meeting commenced. Ruth Watkins, the virologist, was sat at the front table along with Tony and various other people. Several people stood up to ask questions, including what could be done to stop the ongoing culling. There was an atmosphere of quiet panic. Tony read out a poem as an elegy to the animals gone. He wanted to elect a committee. That was the important next step. People raised their hands. Then a farmer from Yorkshire mentioned my name for a potential member of the committee. Tony looked flustered.

I stood up and addressed my comment to Ruth Watkins. I told her that I was very concerned for the hefted sheep up on the Brecon Beacons, as I believed they were in danger of being killed. She gave me a smile and informed me that the sheep were not in danger, as the authorities had promised not to cull sheep with only antibodies. I had no faith in that promise.

Before the meeting ended Tony announced a grand draw. For £5 you could enter for a main prize of a holiday to France. There was a bucket in which to put the money. The money was to be put towards the Group. Christopher Stockdale ended up winning the main prize and he was very pleased. I was glad for him. After the heartache of losing so many of his animals he deserved a holiday.

The main meeting came to a merciful close but we then stayed behind for a discussion of the 'committee'. Discussion turned to the need for a second committee and the issue of FMD seemed to be disappearing fast. I spoke of wishing to tackle the issue from a legal basis, and of the possibility of applying for judicial review, but received such hostility that I was very glad to leave!

The words of one smallholder from Gloucestershire echoed in my thoughts. 'It seems to me that we are fiddling whilst Rome burns', she had said to the people at the 'top table'. I could not have agreed more.

22

The Lion Hotel and More Meetings

On Tuesday 3 July we had a meeting at the Lion Hotel in Builth Wells. Julian, the vet from Somerset, had telephoned me to ask if I would arrange a meeting for farmers, in an attempt to give them support and information. Mr O'Driscoll was the owner of the Lion Hotel and Julian had suggested that the pub would be a good venue. Julian had met Mr O'Driscoll when in Builth Wells at the meeting on 18 June, and he felt that he was on our side. When I phoned Mr O'Driscoll about the proposed meeting he was very enthusiastic. He told me how he had refused accommodation to the military when they had wanted to book into his hotel a few weeks earlier. I had read the newspaper report at the time. Mr O'Driscoll was a rare hotelier, because most seemed to welcome the large bookings.

Mr O'Driscoll greeted us warmly when we arrived at the Lion in early evening. An enormous stone lion guarded the entrance hall. The public bar was quiet but soon it started to fill up with people whose faces I recognised. We had a drink and then Mr O'Driscoll took us to the small room where the meeting was to be held. There were several rows of chairs lined up ready and I began to feel nervous. A long table was at one end and it seemed that the meeting would be of a formal nature unless somehow the chairs could be quickly rearranged. Too late as people were already coming in and taking their places.

Julian arrived from somewhere in the hotel. He looked as if he'd just had a bath and was obviously feeling at home! Christopher Stockdale arrived. He volunteered to be part of the top table. The room filled up and we sat down. Matthew sat next to me, with Glyn at the end. Mr Gatehouse had brought his friend John Staley, also a farmer, and they sat in the front row. I started sorting out the documents, which I had brought, including relevant pages from the 1981 Animal Health Act. A loud voice, instantly recognisable, entered the room and came to sit bang opposite me in the front row. Mr Pratt smiled and I felt horrified.

Mr O'Driscoll had offered us a meal and his wife brought in huge plates of food; fish and chips for Glyn and myself and chicken nuggets with chips for Matthew. So the meeting got underway with Mr Pratt watching us tucking in. It was difficult not to feel highly embarrassed.

Julian took centre stage for most of the meeting, which in one sense was good, because he is quietly persuasive and has experience as a vet. However, even though I myself have Christian beliefs, he can be a little over-powering in his Methodist-like zeal and he began to chide the people sat there for being spiritually asleep. I agreed with him on this but the people of Wales do not take kindly to being told they are asleep, or anything else for that matter. There have to be other ways of making them wake up.

Christopher Stockdale spoke of the cull of his animals and of his views that there needed to be alternatives. I wanted to let the people know about their rights and a particular clause in the 1981 Act relating to compulsory revocation of infected area status upon knowledge that errors in diagnosis have been made. I spoke up and Julian thanked me for this valuable contribution. The chance was there then to tell the farmers about a piece of legislation brought in by the Welsh Assembly on 4 July. It was a regulation, which forbade vaccination by anyone other than the authorities. Farmers around the Brecon Beacons area had requested vaccination and it seemed that this had been brought in to ensure that it was not deemed possible or legal.

There was intense interest from the audience at this point, and then Mr Pratt grabbed the papers. I could almost see him looking for the place to strike. He found it. The booming commenced, which is extremely loud when sat in front of him. I had it all wrong; this was not prohibition of vaccination. It was obvious that the authorities were planning to vaccinate, he said, otherwise they would not have drawn this up to prevent anyone from vaccinating. Mr Pratt looked at me in a triumphant fashion. I stared at him and decided that he was not going to win in his attempts at humiliation. I explained to the farmers that the piece of legislation had only been brought into Wales, not the UK as a whole, and therefore it did appear that the Welsh Assembly was trying to make sure that it would be more difficult for farmers to request vaccination. I tried to point out that it had been brought in immediately following a request from some of the Brecon Beacons graziers. Astonishingly Mr Pratt made no further attempts to shut me up and he left the meeting in apparent good humour towards me.

The formal meeting drew to a close. We said goodbye to various people, including Mr Gatehouse. Most of them felt the meeting had been a good one. The room became more and more empty. I started to pack the papers away. A farmer from Builth Wells introduced me to a vet who worked for the Ministry. I had seen him at one of the previous meetings and had met his wife in the hallway before this meeting. He had knowledge of all the test results for Powys, as he was a senior vet, and he knew that many of the test results were returning as negative, but were being kept as positive on the list. Whilst being aghast at what was happening he feared for the loss of his job and this fear made him fail to make this knowledge public. Vets in the State Veterinary Service across the UK were being forced to do likewise.

We thanked Mr and Mrs O'Driscoll for their hospitality and then drove home, feeling exhausted but pleased that the meeting had generated a good response. Some weeks later Christopher Stockdale told me that Mr Pratt had said that he was going to try and drown me at the meeting, either with words or in the river! Now I understood why he had sat almost nose to nose with me that night, and had tried to prevent me from speaking.

The next and last time we met Mr Pratt was at another meeting on 11 July, again in Builth Wells, in the Montgomery Pavilion at the show-ground. This time Mr Pratt was very polite and congenial, so perhaps he had forgotten to carry on his strange vendetta against me.

That meeting was held to discuss vaccination. Fewer farmers were there than had attended the meeting of 18 June and there was a sense of weariness amongst the audience. Ruth Watkins had come there to present her viewpoint on vaccination and unfortunately she cited the hefted sheep as being a great potential problem in that it was possible that they were the cause of the outbreaks in the cattle. This I knew not to be the case, as the senior vet from Llandrindod Wells had told me that the outbreaks in the cattle had nothing to do with the sheep at all.

Chairing the meeting was Edwin Roderick and next to him was a farmer from the southern area of the Brecon Beacons. He was the vice president of the FUW at the time and has since retired from the position. He seemed somewhat bemused, and as if he had contradictory views. There was genuine anger in him about the mass culling that had taken place in Powys but at the same time he appeared to hold the view that it was necessary. Presumably these contradictions arose due to his being an official with the FUW, which supported the government's culling policy, whilst at the same time being an ordinary farmer fearing for his own livestock.

After Ruth Watkins completed her presentation there was a vote taken on vaccination. Several farmers were against it but a vote in support of vaccination was carried, and it was decided to relay this information to the Welsh Assembly and DEFRA. Mr Pratt spoke out very much in favour of vaccination and made sure that everyone heard him.

As we were leaving I could hear a man asking if a Janet Hughes was there. He was Maurice Vellacott, a farmer from south-west England and we had spoken on the phone several times in recent weeks. Maurice had come to the meeting with David Handley, the dairy farmer from Monmouthshire who had held protests about fuel and milk prices. We had a long chat. Maurice believed that there was a conspiracy to change the use of the land completely and I agreed that the actions of the government were pointing in that direction. David Handley came to say hello and told us that he had been over to Strasbourg and had spoken with David Byrne the EU Commissioner for Farming. David Byrne had apparently informed him that the EU had agreed to vaccination in the UK wherever it was necessary. It was the UK government which was opposing its use; not the EU. Mr Pratt joined us out in the chilly night air and we all agreed that something had to be done to force the government to alter its policy. David Handley wanted to arrange a mass protest. I wondered how much notice this government took of anything. We left and again drove through the disinfectant baths, and off home, unaware of what the next few days were bringing.

23

The Pens

Friday 13 July passed and Saturday arrived. I felt a kind of relief. It was not to last long. The phone rang in the afternoon and it was Mr Gatehouse. He was sounding very heated. They had found foot and mouth at Cwm Llwch he told me. Cwm Llwch is a steep sided valley leading down from Pen y Fan, the highest peak of the Brecon Beacons. I told Mr Gatehouse that I did not believe they had found foot and mouth virus. He had heard that it was virus and that they were planning to test thousands of the sheep up on the Beacons. So here was the mass cull feared by so many.

On 14 July a press announcement of the Welsh Assembly appeared in The Western Mail. The press report confirmed that foot and mouth antibodies had been 'discovered in a sheep grazing on the Brecon Beacons.'

An Assembly spokeswoman was quoted as stating that, 'It is not completely unexpected; this is why we were testing them. We are penning them off, and testing, tagging them and identifying all the sheep. We are dealing with a lot of sheep. We are talking in the region of 10,000 sheep. We are fully aware of what the situation is.'

Antibodies had been found in **a** sheep. One sheep? Why on earth were they suddenly talking of 10,000 sheep? The officials at the Welsh Assembly either had no sense or they were trying to fool the public, not to mention the owners of the sheep. Anger took hold of me.

During the following week four large pens were constructed on the lower slopes of the Beacons, to hold the sheep for testing, so they said. I knew they were killing pens. I did not know what to do. No one knew what to do. It was too hurtful to watch the TV news with the film of the sheep in the pens, but I could hear their cries from the other room whenever the TV news came on. The Welsh Assembly announced to the press that 'While they are in the pens, the farmers will have the chance to shear the sheep and dose them.' Not one of the many thousands of sheep held in those pens came out alive. The 'testing' pens were the pens of death and as soon as the sheep had entered them they may as well have been already dead.

So many phone calls were made to so many farmers over that next week. How I wished that I did not live so far from there. More pens were constructed and news releases from the Welsh Assembly sought to appease the farmers and the public. Carwyn Jones stated that the testing was being undertaken to prove that there was no disease up on the Beacons. It felt though, as if he expected to find disease. In fact, in a letter to the graziers on 13 August 2001, Mr Jones informed them that disease had been spreading from a 'single source' near Pen y Fan. Tony Edwards, the ACVO, wrote of an 'original point' of disease on the Beacons, and that their 'original hypothesis was the correct one as disease' had 'not been found anywhere other than in the immediate area of Pen y Fan.' Why then, the need to cull thousands of sheep from heft areas several miles away from Pen y Fan? I found their comments quite astonishing, because it sounded as if they knew the location of this 'single source' of 'infection.'

The poor trusting animals were kept in the pens for almost two weeks at a time and conditions became very bad for them. Mr Gatehouse told me how he could hear their cries and how he too felt like going to release them. He knew they were healthy; the ewes and their lambs all penned on the hillside and waiting for the farmers to come and let them out. The vets knew they were healthy too but they were just doing a job. However, I do wonder how well they sleep at night.

Wednesday 25 July arrived and with it news that the Welsh Assembly had decided that all 4,000 sheep on that part of the Beacons should be killed as antibodies had been found in a high number of them. That was it; I had had enough. I had been placing messages for help on Sheepdrove and on Wednesday evening a woman from Yorkshire rang up with the name of a solicitor who had helped them in a case in that area. I rang him straight away and said that I was prepared to make an application for an injunction and judicial review. He said that he was able to help, but that he would need £5,000 advance payment. We had savings then and as a family we had made the decision to use them if necessary. None of us could bear what was going on and I think I would have gone mad had I not acted.

Arrangements were made for a draft to be sent to him and he told me that he would sort out the paperwork and get something ready for the next day. When I rang him the following day, 26 July, there was an odd note to his voice. He was now not sure when the paperwork would be ready and he had to have the funds before he could start. Already a day had been wasted and I felt that time was running out for the sheep penned on the slopes. When I rang him later in the day he informed me that he now had another client for the case and therefore was unable to help me. This just did not make sense at all to me. What the devil was going on? Who was this other client and why was this solicitor giving me the cold shoulder?

The picture began to clear. After the solicitor had spoken with me the previous evening, two women had contacted him. These women, who were known to me, had apparently persuaded the solicitor to drop me as a client. They had informed him that they were taking the case forward, together with a farmer from near Welshpool. These same women were the ones who had poured scorn on my suggestions for a judicial review. One of them had telephoned previously, when I had placed a message on the Sheepdrove chat site about the need for a judicial review and told me that 'we have to keep our mouths shut on this Janet.' This had shocked me at the time, and now I felt sure they had no intention of making an application.

The solicitor could tell that I was angry. He said that he would prepare a letter to be sent to Carwyn Jones and that it would be sent the next day at the latest. I asked for his assurance on this. He gave it. The next thing that I knew when I rang him again was that I was not in a position to make an application. I needed to be a farmer. Why then had he agreed to make a case on my behalf when he had been fully aware that I was not a farmer? This was a 'public interest' case, as he was fully aware of, and I had been told that I had a legal entitlement to bring a case, being then a tax- payer and a person residing in Powys. I felt then that he was certainly stringing me along and my temper frayed. Would he or would he not send Carwyn Jones a letter of intent? He would, but it would be better if I could find a farmer. Okay. I would find a farmer. What a silly assumption that was of mine.

That morning the Sarah Dickens programme on BBC Radio Wales, had a special debate called 'What we can believe about Foot and Mouth' and I had been telephoned to ask if I'd take part. I tried to get out the information about sheep with antibodies not being a danger to other animals. Brian Powdrill, Chairman of the Brecon Beacons National Park Authority, was also on the programme, and he cited an open letter, which they had sent to the Welsh Assembly that day, requesting alternatives to culling. If the National Park Authority was publicly requesting alternatives to the slaughter, why on earth was no-one listening? Was it merely a PR exercise?

24

Black Friday

Friday 27 July; a day when hopes were raised only to be dashed on a hard rock. I always hold this date close in my memory, as it is the anniversary of my Mum's death. This year it would be thirty years since I lost her. I wanted the day to bring something good, instead of what it had brought me those years ago.

I rang Mrs Phillips to find out what was happening. They still had their sheep on the mountain, she told me, and had so far not agreed to bring them down. DEFRA and the Welsh Assembly wanted to cull all of those in the pens and their remaining flock on the Beacons, but the Phillips had not agreed to it yet. I told her that I was prepared to take the issue to Court. She sounded elated. I explained that ideally, in order to have sufficient legal interest, a case needed to be brought by a farmer with animals at risk of being culled. I also said that I would be a guarantor if necessary, which would mean that I would be liable for all legal costs if the action failed. She said that she would go and tell the other graziers.

The sheep belonging to the Phillips were apparently being held in the same pen as sheep belonging to the Prossers, who farm on a National Trust property on the lower slopes of the Beacons. I only found out much later that 600 sheep belonging to the Prossers had been tested on 18 July. The results had been negative.

The phone rang an hour or so later. It was Jon Dobson, a man from Hampshire and friend of Alicia Eykyn. He had filmed much of the testing on the Beacons the previous week and was up there again to film further events as they happened. He sounded quite joyous and said that he had heard of my plans and that news was spreading amongst the people there that someone was taking out an injunction. 'You're stopping them Janet!' Was this able to be true? Jon pledged a large amount of money towards the case and rang off. He had been one of the few people involved with the National Foot and Mouth group who had been supportive of my view for the need of a judicial review and I was very glad of his positive thoughts.

Melanie Doyle, from BBC Wales, rang and also Abigail, from HTV, as by this time they too had become aware that I had made a decision to take a case forward. However, there was still the huge problem of the lack of a grazier to be a claimant in an application to the Court. At the moment the threat of an injunction alone seemed to be delaying the slaughter of the sheep and my spirits rose. HTV rang again to ask if I would be able to go down that afternoon to speak at the Storey Arms, which is situated on the A470, the road that runs across the National Park. Sky News was there, Abigail said, and the coverage would go all across the world. I told her that even though I was offering to be guarantor I was having trouble in finding a farmer who would agree to be the claimant and in any case it was impossible to get down to the Beacons that afternoon as Glyn had the car. She rang off, saying that she would ring later on to see if the situation had changed.

The phone rang a little while later and it was Julia Phillips, Mr and Mrs Phillips' daughter. She was so thankful that someone was trying to help, she said. There was desperation in her voice. The officials were trying to force her to gather the sheep off the mountain, she told me, but she was refusing. I told her that I needed a grazier to be the claimant. She said that she would try to persuade her parents or another grazier, but she feared that the other graziers had already signed the consent forms. She did not phone back that day or thereafter. I rang Michaela to ask if she would be a claimant; at least she was a smallholder, if not on the Beacons. She agreed to give it serious consideration if all else failed. Then I rang Nicola, the dairy farmer in Worcestershire. She also said that she would. Well, that would have to do.

Abigail rang again at about 4pm. She said that they had still not started to kill the sheep and there were high hopes that the threat of an injunction was going to prevent them altogether. I had not contacted the solicitor in Yorkshire for fear that he had not sent the letter of intent to Carwyn Jones and I was going to have to bluff my way through it. Abigail asked if I would be able to get to the studio in Mold, North Wales, and I said that I would try, but that it was a fair distance from us. I then rang Glyn's workplace and by chance he had returned from his archaeological site work. I went through events of the day very quickly and asked if he could get home immediately. A short while later a chap from HTV rang to say that they had arranged for a link-up from the studio in Newtown, which made things a good deal easier, as it was only 12 miles away.

We made it to the studio just in time and met Abigail, who made us feel very much at ease. It was to be a live broadcast and I would have to make sure that I spoke up for all those wonderful sheep on the mountain. Nerves simply had to be ignored. The cameraman was coming down from Mold and he was late. Abigail started to worry but then he appeared just moments before the news began. Lucy, the newsreader, had a quick chat with me and she sounded so re-assuring. The item on the sheep was the main story and suddenly they were speaking about it. They interviewed Glyn Pritchard of the FUW, and he said that he was extremely puzzled as to why there was a delay in the sheep being killed. I began to feel anger rising and then there was the cue for me to speak.

Lucy asked me what was happening with the legal situation and I said that I was taking out an injunction and that Carwyn Jones had received a letter before action from a solicitor. I prayed that this was so. There was no disease in any of the sheep, I explained, and healthy animals were being killed. If Carwyn Jones went ahead he would be in breach of the law. The bulletin ended and Abigail gave me a big hug. We made our way back home through the late evening sunshine and watched the recorded news when we reached home. I was surprised that, apart from looking very green on the TV, I had managed to appear fairly composed and had made my intention clear to anyone who wished to hear. Now it was time to wait.

The hours went by and the time came for the late news bulletin. All our prayers and intentions were laid bare and desolate with the news that they had started to kill the sheep at around 8pm. So the graziers had all given in and complied. Bribery and fear had won this day, but there were more days for fighting yet. I felt too upset to cry that night; much the same as I had felt on the night of 27 July 1971, when news came through that my mother had died.

25

Birthday Gifts

The following Sunday, 29 July, was my birthday and I had to try and have a good day for Matthew's sake, as he always finds me such lovely presents.

We knew that more and more sheep were going to be tested on other parts of the Beacons and that the chances were that 'disease' would be found, even if all the animals were as healthy as the day is long.

The phone rang. It was Pat Innocent from the Forest of Dean. She wanted to know how I was getting on and I went over the events of the past few days. She said that she wanted to help and that she would be the applicant if necessary. My spirits started to rise. Pat offered £1,000 to start a case and said that the barrister who had helped her fight MAFF might be worth a try. The barrister has a law firm in Ross-on-Wye and Pat gave me her home number. We had a long conversation but she was unwilling to act for me as a lawyer. She told me that she did not wish to be responsible for my bankruptcy, which she feared would be the outcome of taking on the Government. So that door closed. What was I to try next?

Over recent months I have asked myself over and over again why I did not approach local firms of solicitors. I do not find any sensible answer. My only excuse is that advice came from various professionals that I needed a firm, which was not afraid to be involved in tackling the Government. The firm needed to be a large enterprise. That advice had made sense at the time, but in hindsight it might not have been the best advice.

A woman who I had met at the meeting in Wolverhampton in June has a brother who is a magistrate in South Wales and a few weeks previously had given me his contact details. I had telephoned him shortly after the meeting and he had been very sympathetic of the plight of the farm animals and the affected communities. He told me that he had known Rhodri Morgan for many years and offered to write to him on my behalf. He was as good as his word, but Rhodri Morgan was not moved. Anyway, I decided to phone him again to ask if he could recommend a firm of lawyers. He was at home.

After listening to my plans, and realising that I was not going to change my course, he recommended a firm of solicitors in central Cardiff; Dolmans. He knew one of the partners, Mr MacWilkinson, and said that the firm was efficient and would not be afraid of the Government.

When I rang, Mr MacWilkinson was just off to play golf, but he listened to my intentions, then said that he would have a think about a potential case and get back to me.

Matthew had made sure that I had a very nice birthday cake from Safeways and we had a tea that evening. As I blew out my candles I made a wish.

PART TWO

THE CASE

26

Making a Start

On Monday 30 July Mr MacWilkinson telephoned to say that he was willing to take the case on. Relief and apprehension arrived. He told me that it would be necessary to have a barrister who worked out of Wales, with no connections with the Welsh Assembly. He was going to contact various firms in London. We discussed the potential costs; up to £25,000 for a full judicial review. £25,000. Our long-term savings came to about £12,000 and I felt so desperate that I was prepared to use it all. The remaining amount would have to be met from some other source. I agreed to go ahead with his firm. Dolmans was to take the helm from now on and be my defence against the dark opponent of Government. I told him of Pat as a potential applicant and that fact seemed to bolster his thoughts on the suitability of a case.

Mr MacWilkinson started talking of meeting with a barrister by the end of the week. The test results for the next groups of sheep might be back sooner and culling was on the cards so I wanted to get things started as soon as possible and I explained this to him. So a meeting was arranged for the following day. Mr MacWilkinson was going to contact various Chambers and hopefully an available barrister would emerge in time.

I rang Pat to let her know and we started to make plans to meet and for her to come with us to Dolmans. On the same day there was to be a demonstration outside the Welsh Assembly and Pat was going to that too. I began to worry about someone else finding out about the plans for a case, lest the same sabotage happen as on 27 July. So I said to Pat that I would go alone to the solicitors. Even though I knew she really wanted to be there too I was not taking any chances whatsoever. I just wanted to get the case started and then people could find out.

Tuesday 31 July arrived and nerves set in a bit. The lady who was going to be in charge of the case at Dolmans was Claire Jones, and she rang that morning to let me know that a barrister had been found. He was from a Chambers in Bristol and as yet it was undecided whether he was to come to Cardiff or I had to get to Bristol. She would ring back before we left.

I rang Edwin Roderick, the farmer near the Brecon Beacons, who had been very much against the culling and who had set up the group to fight the burial site on the Epynt. He was in his car on his way to the meeting at Cardiff. I asked him if he knew anyone who was going to take a case, but he didn't. He told me to be careful of what I was getting myself into and conversation ended. Pat would be on her way to Cardiff now too. I wondered if I had been too paranoid in going without her and decided the decision had been more safe than silly.

We were just about ready to leave for the station. As I was going out of the door the phone rang and it was Claire. The barrister would come to Cardiff, so that was good. Our train would get us to Cardiff just in time and no extra rush or journey would be needed. Glyn waved us off at Shrewsbury and Matthew settled down next to me. I shall always remember Matthew's solidarity with me on the many stressful occasions that were to confront us. He must have secretly feared many of them but throughout he quietly and patiently stood by and supported me. Without his quiet presence I wonder if my nerve would have failed.

The outlines of Cardiff appeared and the train slowly came to a halt. The ship-like Millennium Stadium towered above the roof-tops of the shops and seagulls floated by. A short taxi-drive and we were in Windsor Place; a pleasant street lined with trees and smart terraces. Behind lime trees and beyond the wide pavement was Dolmans; a large mellow pink-brick building. Oh dear, it all looked very expensive. Timidly we went in and introduced ourselves to the smart woman at the reception desk. Claire would be along shortly. We sat in the large soft chairs and I tried not to feel awkward. Thoughts of the sheep mixed with the paintings on the cream walls. I picked up a glossy folder, which held leaflets describing the role of Dolmans in the legal society of the City of Cardiff. A young woman came down the stairway and towards us. Claire Jones smiled and shook hands. She seemed to look for someone else. No, just Matthew and me.

She led us to a small room and closed the door. We sat down around the conference-type table and the issue of payment arose immediately. A cheque for £2,000, as agreed, was to be handed over and then she would ring Leslie Blohm, the barrister from Bristol. I think that I might have been wise to have left at that stage in view of the cheque business but I was so desperate to get things started that I do think I would have handed over my life's possessions had someone asked then. Later demands would be a very different matter.

Cheque duly signed, Claire Jones whisked it away. On the table there were several pieces of paper and being nosy I went through them. They contained information on several barristers, including Leslie Blohm. Details of their expertise were given together with their photograph and fees and I saw that one of Mr Blohm's fields of expertise was in agriculture. He looked very young in the photograph.

Claire Jones came back in the room and quickly gathered the papers together and put them into her file. She looked agitated to see that she had left them where I could read through them. Anyway, discussion started and the salient facts were written into her file. She had printed off information from the Western Mail and there was a statement that more sheep were to be culled. I was frantically trying to think which groups of sheep these might be. Where was the grazier, she wanted to know? This turned into a problem, as I feared it would. Hadn't I been supposed to be bringing someone with me? Yes, but change of plan. Oh well, it would just have to be like this for now, but highly unsatisfactory, because I did not have the legal standing to bring a case.

I had brought with me the book containing the many phone numbers of the graziers in the Brecon Beacons and this seemed to cheer Claire Jones a little. She said that I could telephone them from the phone in the room in order to try and find someone willing to be an applicant. I told her of Pat, but she was not grazing sheep on the Beacons and was therefore not suitable either. Claire went off and left me to ring round. First came Brian Powdrill, Chairman of the Brecon Beacons National Park. He sounded very friendly and said that I had gone out on a limb and it was very brave, and he did give me a few names of possible candidates. However, I could tell that he thought it very unlikely that any of them would agree to the proposal. He was right; no one wanted to become involved and even though the voices on the other end of the phone tried to sound convincingly concerned they held the tones of bewildered astonishment that I should even be contemplating such action.

Claire Jones returned. The barrister had arrived. She took us to another small room filled with a table piled with thick volumes, behind which a fairly young man sat. We were introduced to Leslie Blohm and after brief pleasantries he launched into a two-hour long investigation of the merits of a case. Just as I was beginning to feel that he believed a case to be without shred of hope, he became a different man. He told me that if I could find a grazier, willing to be the applicant, then he Leslie Blohm would get out of bed in the middle of the night if necessary and take the paper work in his pyjamas to an available judge. Well, what a turn up! We shook hands and I thanked him for the inquisition, then we said our farewells to Claire and the receptionist behind the desk. Out we went into the late afternoon sunshine. No taxi but a slow walk back to city centre for a meal.

In one of the main streets a fairground had set up and there was a carousel whirling round. My hopes were rising. If Leslie Blohm believed there to be a case, then perhaps there was real hope. We went into a cafe and tucked into our food, then made the rest of the walk to the station for our train. I rang Glyn to let him know the time of our train and full of weariness but also raised spirits we went home.

27

Ten Sheep

The next morning, 1 August, I rang Claire Jones to make sure she was writing to Carwyn Jones with my intentions. She was sending a letter that day, she said, and faxed me a copy. So at least that first step had happened this time. Abigail from HTV rang, wanting to know what was happening. She wanted to do a news piece on it she said. So that afternoon she and Phil, the cameraman, came round and took various shots of me at home doing various things, including faxing the letter to Mr Jones. Artistic licence!

The pace of events started to grow slowly; much too slowly for me. I wanted to get into Court and get the evil stopped. However, until a grazier was found nothing could happen. That day and subsequent days I rang round every farmer possible in the Brecon Beacons area. Claire Jones sent me a sheet of possibilities, gleaned from somewhere, but there was no one, seemingly, who would take the risk. In the end though, one man, a smallholder with a handful of sheep, said, 'Yes' and I could have hugged him. Claire Jones started the legal ball rolling but hours later the man had phoned back to say he had changed his mind. His wife would not let him do it. This in spite of my offer to stand as guarantor and bear all the financial risk. I despaired at that point and the anger grew.

On 2 August I rang Edwin Harris to find out what was happening down there. He was in fairly friendly mood, even if slightly defensive. I asked him about the test results and he gave me a lot of information. So few of any of the sheep had had positive results and there was one piece of information, which was highly significant. He told me that a group of 159 sheep, belonging to various graziers, had been penned for 14 days on 28 June. The first test had shown one anti-body positive sheep. All the sheep were then killed on 13 July and re-tested. The results had returned the same; just one anti-body sheep. But this meant they must have known there was no active infection. Edwin Harris agreed.

He went on to tell me how he had been kept out of a meeting in Brecon barracks. The meeting had been called by Carwyn Jones and Tony Edwards, the Chief Vet for Wales, had been there too. Edwin Harris had gone along, even though he did not have any sheep up on the Brecon Beacons. All his sheep from the valley had been culled at the end of June. He was, though, Chairman of the Graziers' Association and therefore had an interest in attending the meeting. He was refused entry by Army personnel, but eventually managed to get in, by which time all the graziers had signed the forms of consent. Edwin Harris told me that he had no idea why he was kept out of the meeting, but I wonder if it was because someone was worried that he might say something, which would prevent the graziers from agreeing to the culls. It all sounded very sinister.

At this meeting the Prossers, whose sheep had been held in the same pen as the Phillips' sheep, had been told by Government officials that all of their hefted sheep had to die. One of their sheep held in the pen had apparently tested positive for antibody. On 28 July, Mr Prosser had to order his dog to round up the sheep and lead them some 2 miles over the mountain slopes to the killing pens by the Storey Arms. Samples from these 600 sheep, the same as those tested on 18 July, again returned negative test results. There seems little justification for the authorities to have ordered their slaughter, in the full knowledge that test results had already returned as negative.

That evening I checked the web site of the Welsh Assembly and discovered that a piece of new legislation had been made on 31 July 2001. It was legislation relating to valuations of animals, and all previous valuation amounts had been revoked. This effectively paved the way for an open cheque-book, through which to bribe the graziers even more.

Friday, 3 August came and went and still no grazier had been found. Saturday, 4 August, loomed and with it the fear of more culling. Andrew North from BBC Radio 4 'World at One' rang in the morning to ask if I could get to speak with him later that day. He was down at Brecon but we arranged to meet at Llandrindod Wells, which was striking distance for us all. A few minutes later a reporter from HTV rang to ask if I knew how to get hold of Dr Ruth Watkins. I had her number, which I gave to the woman, but I knew she was unavailable as she was up in Cumbria giving talks. The reporter then asked about a legal case, and seemed to think that Dr Watkins was taking a case. I wondered if she was confusing me with Janet Bayley, often in the company of Ruth Watkins. So I mentioned that I was taking a case and then it turned out that she had found the right Janet after all. Could a cameraman come round? I told her that I had a meeting arranged with Andrew North and she said that she would send Phil, the cameraman, around as soon as possible. He arrived around noon and did a quick interview amongst the roses in the sunshine of our garden.

Then it was a quick dash down to Llandrindod Wells and the Metropole. We parked the car in the hotel car park and wandered round to the front entrance. So this was the place where the army, vets and slaughter-men were staying. As we stood in the foyer a tall young man came up to us and introduced himself as Andrew North. We had a long talk and he taped our conversation on a balcony at the back of the hotel. He told us how he had watched the groups of vets and slaughter-men and the army personnel, and how awful he found the whole business.

He was very positive about what I was trying to achieve and wished us well as he left. I felt wobbly with tiredness and anxiety and before we left I glanced around the room next to the balcony. A tapestry picture caught my attention. The picture was of a man in a long robe, seated in a large formal chair and in front of him someone was kneeling, pleading. It was like a symbol of the judge who was to decide the fate of the sheep.

I had no sheep, even though the Daily Post carried a piece stating that a teacher was trying to 'save her flock'. It felt like the sheep on the Brecon Beacons were my sheep. Their owners seemed to have disowned them and this was the tragedy. As my solicitor was to say repeatedly, it only needed a grazier to say 'No' and the whole thing would stop. This was Mr John Wilkins' view and I believed he was correct.

Mr Wilkins took over the case from Claire Jones when she went on holiday and he stayed on the case until funds ran out. He is a very nice, personable man, with a kind heart, but Dolmans is not a charity and Mr Wilkins is a partner at Dolmans; not my benefactor. Therefore his kindness had to be tempered with company procedure. At one point he apparently told a lawyer in another firm that the case was making him dream of sheep. That was in September and it was not until 10 August that we met Mr Wilkins.

On 6 August I had an email from a retired barrister in Lancashire. She suggested that I purchase sheep and take the case myself. What a grand idea! When I told Claire Jones of this she said that she had tried to tell me this. Oh. Right. Now I must find a farmer willing to sell me some sheep. Farmers would surely relish the chance to sell their unwanted animals.

7 August came and went, and no farmer had been found. Sue Goddard, the Western Mail reporter, put in a piece about my search for sheep but by the afternoon of 8 August there was still no farmer willing to sell me some of his or her sheep. I rang Brian Bowen, who farms on the southern part of the Brecon Beacons and he said that he would ask his father. His father spoke with me on the phone and his first eager tones of a possible Yes changed soon to a No. It was all too risky apparently. He said that he would ask around, but the result was the same. I rang Mr Gatehouse. His eldest daughter's boyfriend worked on a farm near Talybont-on-Usk and he said that he would ask them if they would sell me some sheep.

Ten minutes later Mr Gatehouse rang back. Yes the Williams would sell me some sheep! He gave me their number and Mr Williams answered. Yes he would sell me some of his sheep. How many would I like? Oh. I thought a small number because later on it might prove a problem as we only have quarter of an acre at home. He solved it all. Ten sheep would be a good number; five ewes and five lambs. He said that he would buy them back afterwards if necessary and if I had been next to him he would have received a big kiss! Two days and many farmers later and at last a farmer who was not afraid to sell me his sheep.

A purchase price was sorted out and suddenly I had ten sheep and the legal standing to make an application for a judicial review against the Welsh Assembly. Mr Williams never cashed my cheque in payment for the sheep and he also sent in £500 towards funding for the case. He was one farmer who made me feel that I was not embarking on a worthless path.

28

Donors and Drunks

The idea for the Save Our Sheep Fund had come about as Matthew and I were in our back garden. He was on his climbing frame and I was having a sit on the bench. We were trying to think of how to manage all the costs of a case and the idea of a fund for donations sprang to mind. Then Matthew suggested the name; Save Our Sheep, SOS for short. Pat from Gloucestershire started the account up with her large donation and over the coming months we were to be absolutely amazed at the generosity and compassion of hundreds of people the length and breadth of Britain.

Ironically our village was silent on the issue and maintained this silence throughout. That is one aspect that I shall never understand and never forget. However, the kindness and compassion of so many people who I shall never have the chance to meet overwhelmed us. Various papers in Wales carried the story of the case and placed details of the fund. We were thrilled when the first donation arrived in the post; it was from Mrs Williams, a farmer from Brooks, near Berriew, with words of encouragement. People started to phone up with offers of help. A farmer from Snowdonia was so relieved that someone was taking a case that he broke down and cried over the phone.

Envelopes addressed to 'Save Our Sheep Fund' started to pour in; some contained cheques and some contained bank notes. The accompanying letters held such encouraging words that it was impossible to feel anything else than positive about the case. Complete strangers seemed to have such faith in the case that it could not fail.

Friday, 10 August arrived. At 10.58am an email arrived from Mr Wilkins urging me to get down to Cardiff ASAP as he had a barrister coming over from Bristol that afternoon. So it was then a mad dash to Shrewsbury for the train.

Abigail from HTV kept in contact on the mobile and told me that a car would meet us and take us to Dolmans. She was so excited about the possibility of an injunction actually happening, but I told her that it might not. It was not definite. It all depended on the opinion of the barrister. Nevertheless, a car would still meet us. Whilst on the train a reporter from the Telegraph rang to ask how things were going. He too sounded elated. I was very apprehensive and kept silently telling myself not to expect too much.

We arrived at Cardiff Station. It was now about 2pm. As we walked out onto the paved forecourt a fair-haired girl called from a smart car. It was Tanya from HTV and another reporter. We got in and I directed them to Dolmans. I explained that it was not certain that anything would happen today; it all depended on what the barrister decided. We arrived outside Dolmans and Tanya said that they would wait for us in the bar at the end of the road. She had hoped to film the meeting but it was not possible. So we went inside and sat down to wait for Mr Wilkins.

A grey-haired man came quickly down the staircase and walked over to us, hand outstretched. He told us that the barrister had arrived, so we followed Mr Wilkins into a room overlooking the street. At the large table sat Guy Adams, yet another barrister who was to make a decision on the merits of the case. Leslie Blohm had not been available so Guy Adams was the chosen one. After brief introductions we all sat down. A young dark-haired man sat down opposite. Mr Wilkins introduced him as Bryn Thomas, his clerk. Mr Wilkins sat down at the end of the table and the meeting commenced.

Guy Adams had a pile of books in front of him, like Leslie Blohm, and was earnestly trying to digest the relevant facts. He was very quiet indeed and I felt unable to ask questions for the time being. He surfaced from the paperwork briefly and advised Mr Wilkins to arrange for a fax to be sent to DEFRA legal department in London to inform them that an injunction was planned and to request that the culling planned for the coming weekend be stopped. This was sent at 2.44pm. The letter that had been sent to Carwyn Jones on 1 August had resulted in DEFRA demanding to be kept informed. The Welsh Assembly had refused to take any responsibility for the culling. DEFRA had sent numerous faxes to Dolmans since 2 August insisting that they be told if or when an application was made to the Court.

Tanya rang, wondering what was happening. Mr Wilkins looked very disapprovingly at my mobile phone and I tried to explain to Tanya that so far not much progress had been made but that a fax had been sent to DEFRA in London informing them of the intention for an injunction. The call ended with her saying that they would still wait to find out.

At last, Guy Adams looked up from the documents and an intense discussion began. He needed to be convinced of a case because from what he had seen so far he was not convinced. So I had to make my case before him as I had with Leslie Blohm. Tea and coffee arrived on a tray and Bryn poured everyone's choice. He seemed as bemused as I was with it all. Mr Wilkins peered over his reading spectacles periodically and made notes. Bryn made copious notes.

Meanwhile a reply arrived from DEFRA. The writer sounded arrogant and as if their rights had been infringed by this upstart from the countryside. No they were not prepared to agree to halt the culling and they were not prepared to provide details of testing procedure or results. They wanted to know if I had any sheep due to be culled. My ten sheep near Talybont-on-Usk were amongst a large flock grazing somewhere on the Beacons but I did not know their precise location so I was unable to know if they were to be amongst those to be culled. DEFRA's letter stated that the graziers had all consented to the cull that weekend. What a mess this was turning into.

My mobile rang again and Mr Wilkins looked at me severely. The reporters would have to leave. The meeting could not be interrupted for reporters. Okay. I told Tanya that I would come out to see them and explain the situation. I walked to the bar at the end of Windsor Place. Tanya and the other reporter were outside holding glasses. Oh, how I wanted to join them. She looked very deflated when I said that it looked unlikely that an injunction could be taken out that day. I told her that apparently the owners of the sheep to be culled that weekend had all signed the consent forms and therefore there was nothing legally that I was able to do. One of the graziers would have to make the application if the cull was to be stopped. It was all so disappointing. I told her that I would let them know if something did happen and she said they would still wait a little longer.

I went back up the street and into Dolmans, then back into the room with the conference table. Guy Adams looked hot and uncomfortable. Discussion resumed. Matthew sat there taking it all in. Correspondence was faxed back and forth with DEFRA as Guy Adams struggled to find the bones of a case. I brought out any aspect that I could think of about why it was so wrong for the sheep to be culled. They were all healthy and the finding of antibodies to foot-and-mouth showed that they were immune to it. Guy Adams still seemed to be unconvinced about the strength of the argument but Mr Wilkins was looking positive. He said that I did not have to convince him; I was knocking on an open door. Suddenly Guy Adams' stance changed. Yes he had an idea. Thank goodness for that I thought, with great relief. The hours had gone by unnoticed really and it was getting on for 6pm. How much longer would this take? The HTV reporters had phoned to say they had to leave and I could hear the huge disappointment in Tanya's voice. I felt that I was somehow letting her down too. Stupid I know, but it felt like that.

Guy Adams had apparently found something to make sufficient legal argument. Thank God. The penning for testing, he felt, was giving an opportunity to make sure whether disease was present or not but they were culling in spite of the penning, before final test results were known. Irrational. Yes, here were grounds for an argument, he now believed. The room shot to life and people started scuttling back and forth. Bryn Thomas disappeared and returned with a laptop and this was positioned at another table. Guy Adams had some more coffee and then went off to sit at the laptop. Matthew and I smiled at one another and the atmosphere of despair changed to one of total optimism. Here was a case. Here was a barrister who would now lead us to victory. He had finally been convinced and I wondered if he too would get up in the middle of the night to go to a judge. I phoned Glyn to let him know we were still in Cardiff and he sounded tense. I could not tell him much except that the barrister seemed positive and that we would be home as soon as possible.

Guy Adams tapped away at the laptop and then I was asked to go and sit with him. He wanted to know my details to place in the argument. Environmental science teacher; was there such a thing? Of course there was! The requirement to be a tax-payer cropped up. Public interest case. Concerned member of the public. Oh well it would have to suffice. Don't forget my ten sheep. Guy Adams wrote the outline of an argument and time passed.

Mr Wilkins asked me to go with him to sort something out. Matthew came too. I glanced at my watch and was shocked to discover that it was nearly 9pm. I must phone Glyn soon. We followed Mr Wilkins to a room down the corridor and he closed the door. The walls were lined with rows of legal volumes and Mr Wilkins drew up a chair. The matter of money had to be covered. Oh of course. I had my cheque-book in my bag in anticipation of this. How much did they require? Mr Wilkins made it his duty to warn me of vast expenditure. He was aware that we are not affluent people but that we had savings. I had this complete faith that financial help would come in and I told him about the fund. There would be need of a further £10,000 up to a hearing. £10,000 was a huge amount to us but seemed little in comparison to the lives of the poor sheep. I wrote out two cheques, each for £5,000 and Mr Wilkins deftly placed them in the drawer.

The room grew darker as he told me that he did not think it was going to be possible to make an application for an injunction for this coming weekend with all the graziers concerned having signed the forms of consent. I was dismayed. He said that he believed that I would be granted a judicial review though, and that I would have to view this coming weekend's cull as a sacrifice in order to get the whole matter to a review stage for all the remaining sheep. But we had come all this way down to Cardiff to take action today. Yes he knew this. It was all very sad but it was just not legally possible to take out an injunction if the owners of the sheep had agreed to them being culled. I felt absolutely gutted. We returned to the conference room.

Mr Wilkins went over to talk with Guy Adams, who was still at the laptop. What was going to happen now? He confirmed Mr Wilkins' words. It was just not possible to go to a Court this evening to take out an injunction. All the graziers had agreed to the cull and this fact had thrown the whole procedure awry. I wanted to plead with them but could see that it was impossible to save the sheep this weekend. They were already dead on paper. I felt terrible anger at the graziers, many of whom knew of my offer to take legal action. Why had they consigned their wonderful healthy animals to this cruel death?

The way forward was to get an application in early the following week, for both an injunction and judicial review. Mr Wilkins was trying to decide what to do about DEFRA. The lawyer there, Jon Townsley, was still in his office, waiting to hear the decision. Mr Wilkins paced up and down the room. The Welsh Assembly should be the main party to the case but it was

DEFRA who were waiting for the phone call. Mr Wilkins phoned Mr Townsley. He told him that an injunction would not be happening this weekend but that an application would be made at the beginning of next week. Mr Wilkins held his mobile aloft and spoke firmly to Mr Townsley. The fact of the consent by the graziers was mentioned and the call ended with Mr Wilkins saying joyously, 'Well the forms will be served on you then Jon'. The call ended at 10pm.

Guy Adams had started to pack away all his many books into a little case on wheels. Mr Wilkins asked if he could ring up for train times for us and this he did. Guy Adams' train to Bristol was due in half an hour or so, but there were apparently no more trains going to Shrewsbury that night. Oh my God. We had been at Dolmans for eight hours and I had completely forgotten to check when the last train would leave. Mr Wilkins suggested a B&B. No we had to get back home. Mr Wilkins phoned the help-line again. There was a train to Hereford at mid-night and there was a bus to Craven Arms because the lines were up. Oh Hereford would be great. A taxi was called and all three of us piled in. Mr Wilkins waved us off and the taxi-driver seemed bemused at us leaving the office of a solicitor's at so late an hour. Perhaps he thought there had been an office party. Guy Adams paid the fare and we all ambled into the station. We were very hungry and queued up in Burger King. There was quiet embarrassment between us with Guy Adams keeping a reserved mental distance. He was after all a barrister. He bought his take-away and made to leave. As he was going he smiled and said that it would be good for the forms to be served on Mr Jones. A large seagull flew past and I hoped he was right.

I bought some burgers with fries and drinks, and went to sit down by Matthew. We ate but we were both so tired. Midnight was still a long way off and we grew more and more miserable. We sat there until 11.30pm, then made our way up to the platform. The air felt chilly because we were tired I expect. We went to sit down. Seagulls came to look at us to see if we had any food for them. Policemen started to appear and we wondered why. A few moments later and the platform began to be filled up with an avalanche of people worse for the wear with drink. I went to ask a station officer if we were on the correct platform. He said that in a few minutes the platform number would be altered just before the train arrived in order to prevent problems with the drunks. He gave us the number and told us to go quietly over there. A woman came over to us to ask what was going on, as she was worried too. So I told her about the imminent platform change. The train arrived and the large group of drunken people started to move up and across the metal stairs like a tidal wave. The presence of policemen made me feel tense. What did they expect? I had never been at Cardiff station at midnight before and I so wanted to be home. Poor Matthew was worn out but was being so brave that I felt very proud of him indeed.

At last we were in our seats and the train was moving off. Slurred voices and the crash of cans accompanied us to Hereford, with a few getting off the train at Abergavenny. Nervously Matthew and I followed the wobbling line of people to a small bus, which was to take us to Craven Arms. The bus filled up to the brim, mostly with drunken people. It then set off with a lurch and the swearing started. 2am on 11 August and here we were on our way through the Herefordshire countryside in a busload of drunks. Matthew gazed out of the window as the swearing increased. Enough was enough, surely. I was fed up anyway and this was just too much. I went up to the driver and asked him if he could request that the swearing passengers be asked to stop their swearing. It was getting to Matthew and having paid our fare for a train journey it did not seem right for us to be subjected to dozens of drunken, cavorting people. Nervously I returned to my seat and mercifully the swearing subsided at the request of the driver. The people seemed to sober up as soon as they were reminded that there was a child present.

Leominster appeared and most of the drunks got off the bus there. Then Ludlow was next and they had all gone. Thank the Lord for that. I just wanted my bed and Matthew was nearly out of his head with tiredness. The bus trundled on and at last reached Craven Arms. As the driver swung the bus round into the road to the station we spotted Glyn in a phone box. He looked very glad when he heard us calling him. It was 2.45am and we were so thankful when we were in the car on the way home. By 3.30am we were home and 4am saw us tucked up in our beds. Relief to be home; despondency at the failure to take out an injunction. Sleep.

29

The Judge's Decision

We had a fairly quiet weekend but I was haunted by the knowledge that thousands more sheep were being killed. I spoke with more graziers, including Mrs Phillips again, and told her of the application planned for Monday. She told me that Mr John Phillips, a relative of her husband, was trying to fight the cull of his sheep. He had 3,000 on a heft to the east of the main peaks of Pen-y-Fan and Corn Ddu. So far he had refused to sign the form. How I wished that I had known of this on Friday, because Jon Townsley had been wrong when he wrote that all graziers concerned had signed the consent forms.

The television news reported the situation on the Beacons throughout the weekend. A mist descended on the Sunday and gathering of sheep had to be postponed. I prayed that the mist would last until an application went into the courts on Monday. Carwyn Jones was reported as being highly annoyed by the mist, and I was thrilled that the culling plans were being thwarted by the power of nature.

The mists stayed until Monday and Mr Phillips still had his sheep. He had not signed their death warrant and when I spoke with him he was adamant that he was not going to let them go. He knew they were healthy and he would fight he told me.

Mr Wilkins was organising the forms and rang to say that they would be faxing them through for me to sign. Guy Adams's argument was being finalised and it was hoped that an application would be made that day. The forms came through in the afternoon at 4.30 pm. The heading for my witness statement held the name of the National Assembly for Wales as the defendant and I was glad that DEFRA was out of the legal frame. It was not going to be possible to get the forms to court until Tuesday 14 August

Mr Wilkins told me. Oh no. More delays. I tried to be patient but I told him of the current situation on the Beacons and of Mr John Phillips. Definitely the next day I was told.

Tuesday 14 August dawned. We were going to Shrewsbury to transfer the savings into our bank so that the cheques to Dolmans would not bounce. Abigail from HTV rang and told me that she had heard that sheep were being killed next to the road that goes down to Ystradfellte. I was as aghast as she sounded. This area was 5 miles or so west of the central area of the Brecon Beacons so what on earth were they up to now? Mr Wilkins phoned and he had heard this news also. He was however in buoyant mood. The forms were all ready to go to court. I told him we were on our way to Shrewsbury and he said that he would keep in contact and let me know as soon as the application was in court. He was as good as his word and rang as we were in the car and again when we arrived in Shrewsbury. The forms had gone into the court; the forms had been served on the Welsh Assembly. The forms had also been sent to DEFRA. Oh dear. Anyway it was now a matter of time and all that could be done now was await the judge's decision. The main stage of serving the forms had been accomplished and that fact sounded so good that I had to be satisfied.

Wednesday arrived and with it very bad news. John Phillips had given in. Glyn had phoned to see how things were and he told him that he had decided that he could not fight any longer. What had happened to remove his strong fighting spirit? I later found out from Mrs Phillips that Carwyn Jones had held a private meeting with Mr Phillips and this meeting had resulted in him signing the consent forms. Mr Phillips had then been told to gather his flocks into pens previously used for killing sheep and that whatever the blood test results, he would not be allowed to take his sheep back to the hill or down to his in-bye land on his farm. This was evil.

By Thursday 16 August I had lost heart. Nearly all the sheep on the higher slopes of the Brecon Beacons had been lost to the evil slaughter and I felt that I was achieving nothing. The phone rang constantly with people asking what was happening; HTV, Radio Shropshire, and interested members of the public. I had little to tell them except that I was waiting to hear from the court in London.

I spoke with Brian Bowen, the farmer from Rhymney. He had agreed to make a witness statement in support of my case and Bryn Thomas was taking the papers up to his farm. Brian Bowen spoke of the meeting that was arranged for that day at the barracks in Brecon. Carwyn Jones and Tony Edward, the chief vet for Wales, were coming to meet with a large group of graziers. He believed it was a meeting arranged to coerce the next batch of graziers into signing over their sheep and Mr Wilkins was of the same opinion.

I went upstairs in the afternoon and lay on the bed. Glyn came up and said that Mr Wilkins was on the phone. Mr Wilkins told me that he had been trying to contact me for hours. The judge had ordered a hearing as soon as possible. I could not believe it; a hearing? Yes. Things would now move on rapidly Mr Wilkins said, and I must be ready to go to Cardiff or London any day now. My spirits soared but I thought of the thousands of sheep that had gone. A hearing could not get them back. However, the future had to be put first and the past had to be placed somewhere else for the time being. The wonderful news was that the application had not been refused. I wanted to shout it out everywhere. The fax of the judge's order came through from Dolmans at 5.20 pm that evening and I kept looking at it just to make sure it was real.

The TV news carried a story of the meeting at Brecon barracks. The news was that the meeting had been cancelled because neither Carwyn Jones nor Tony Edwards had appeared. I spoke with Brian Bowen in the evening and he told me what had happened. He had gone along to the barracks and waited along with several other graziers and members of the public who had come to demonstrate together with the TV cameras and newspaper reporters. They had waited and waited and then it had become clear that Mr Jones and Mr Edwards were not going to turn up. Brian Bowen said that they were later given the excuse that Mr Jones had refused to go along because the secretary of one of the Graziers' Associations was a solicitor. Guy Adams later said that the real reason that Carwyn Jones had not turned up was that he had found out about the judge's decision that same day. As a barrister himself, Mr Jones would have known the line beyond which he could not cross and would have been well aware that the coercion of the graziers was not legal. We felt great elation at the news of the cancelled meeting and for the first time in weeks we felt able to relax.

Mr Wilkins informed me on Friday 17 August that the hearing was to be held at the High Court in London. It was only later that I read the letter from DEFRA to the court requesting that a hearing be transferred from Cardiff to London. DEFRA had succeeded in hijacking the case.

During the weekend of 18 and 19 August we tried to rest as much as possible and prepared to leave for London on the following Monday. I let Pat and Dafydd know of the hearing and they were both very pleased and said that they would be at the hearing too for support. The summer season in London made hotel booking difficult and the hotel in Ebury Street, where we had stayed in April, had no vacancies. So I settled for a room at the Enrico Hotel in Warwick Way and Pat managed to book a room in a hotel near to us in the same street. It was now a matter of waiting for the decision of the judge.

30

Morning in Court

Mr Justice Stanley Burnton took his place under the Royal Coat of Arms and the hearing began. Guy Adams stood up and addressed the court. After the formal introductions he thanked the judge for listing the matter at such short notice. He explained that prior to the weekend there was an exchange of correspondence between DEFRA and the 'claimant' in which DEFRA had said that they had no present plans for culling. Perhaps their plans had been postponed, I thought, after Carwyn Jones' failure to obtain the necessary signed forms of consent from the graziers.

Guy Adams then apologised for the papers coming in to the judge in 'fits and starts.' Judge Burnton said that he was not quite sure which bundle he was intended to have. Guy Adams informed him that he should have a 'claimant's bundle, my Lord.' Oh this was getting off to a slow start. I grew concerned that the judge may not have read the evidence contained within the documents submitted on my behalf. He did not even seem to know if he had received them.

Eventually all the relevant bundles were found. Then the judge wanted to know if the case was continuing against the Welsh Assembly. The barrister for the Assembly was a Welsh man who works from chambers in London, and he appeared to be terribly angered by Guy Adams' remarks of withdrawing the Assembly from the case with no order for costs. There then followed much ado about whether or not the Assembly should be involved and whether there had been unlawful delegation from DEFRA to the Assembly. Apparently the Assembly had stated that they were happy to be bound by any decision of the court, in relation to DEFRA, and would have withdrawn with no order for costs but had then changed their minds.

Guy Adams was caught off-guard and seemed unsure of his grounds for having the Assembly included. The judge intervened.

'Presumably he (Assembly barrister) wants his costs.'

The Welsh barrister quickly spotted his chance.

'Yes, my Lord, it is worse than that. As I understand my friend, he is saying that the National Assembly did take the decision and he is saying that that involved the exercise of unlawfully delegated powers.'

Very crossly he ended by stating: 'We want our costs anyway now.'

He seemed personally affronted by the fact that the Assembly had been included in the case and during the hearing he grew very red-faced indeed.

Guy Adams said that he was content to continue with both parties, as the evidence showed that the National Assembly had been taking decisions and should be injuncted. Judge Burnton started talking about ball games and said that Guy Adams should have made a decision to include the Assembly or not before playing this 'particular ball game'. It seemed right that the Assembly be included because otherwise, according to the judge, they would only be bound by a decision of the court if they were a party to the proceedings. So there it was. At last Guy Adams was able to start on his legal argument against the mass culls on the Beacons that had occurred in preceding weeks.

I was impressed by how much of the science he had digested. He explained to the court the difference between the various tests for FMD; the ELISA Test for anti-bodies, which is liable to throw up a lot of false positives, and the Virus Neutralisation Test, a more reliable test for anti-bodies. He also mentioned the probang test, which is a test for active virus. The judge asked for the name again.

'P R O B A N G'. Guy Adams spelt it out, and the judge said that he understood that it was done immediately before or after slaughter. Guy Adams confirmed this and said that there was no reason why the test could not be carried out when the animal was being initially tested. It was truly ludicrous that DEFRA was only testing for live virus when the animal was due to be killed or when it was dead. It boiled down to a poor excuse to kill on a mass scale.

Professor Brown had agreed to be a main witness for scientific argument. Mr Wilkins had faxed him over the relevant forms and Professor Fred had duly signed and faxed them back. It was difficult for him to properly comment on the situation with DEFRA putting the evidence in only a few hours before the hearing. However, on the slim body of evidence that had been given to him he had produced a statement of a professional's opinion that went against the mass culling.

DEFRA's ploy of putting the evidence in so late was cunning and should not have been allowed by the courts. Each party has to be given reasonable time in which to inspect evidence from the opponent and had the parties been anyone other than a government department this procedure of putting in evidence so late would surely not have been accepted. But it was.

Whilst listening to Guy Adams and the judge I was trying to digest the evidence in Mr Scudamore's witness statement. He is the Chief Veterinary Officer of the State Veterinary Service and due to retire in March 2004. His signed witness statement was lengthy. I turned to page six and quickly read down the page, where the paragraphs were summarising the IPs in the valley:

'a) IP 1779 at Modrydd, on which FMD was confirmed in cattle on 23 June 2001. Foot and mouth disease virus type O was isolated from epithelium samples submitted on 24 June and from 6 out of 57 blood samples taken from sheep on the premises;

b) IP 1796 at Twynneuadd, contiguous to IP 1779. Twenty one sheep out of 290 tested on the farm were reported antibody positive on 2 July 2001;

c) IP 1801 at Gronfelin, contiguous to IP 1779. One out of 24 tested on the farm was reported antibody positive on 30 June 2001; IP 1806 at Court Gilbert, contiguous to IP 1779. One out of 40 in-bye sheep on the farm were reported antibody positive on 2 July 2001;

d) IP 1789 at Llwynbedw, further towards the Brecon Beacons. This IP was contiguous both to IP 1779 and the common grazing area of the Brecon Beacons. Seropositive results on 29 June 2001 indicated a very high prevalence of FMD: 65 out of 67 sheep in one group, and 15 out of 41 sheep in another group were seropositive and within this group virus was also isolated from 12 of the 41 tested. It is believed that the sheep on these premises were the primary source of infection in the valley and infected the cattle on IP 1779.'

A group of hefted sheep on the Brecon Beacons

'Common Land Closed' – Brecon Beacons National Park

Us with 'Bess'.

Two lorry drivers on stand-by in the lay-by near 'Storey Arms'.

The doomed sheep on the slopes near 'Storey Arms'.

© Press Association

The panic of the pens.

© Press Association

Pen-y-Fan and Corn Ddu, Brecon Beacons.

After the Hearing, 21st August, 2001.

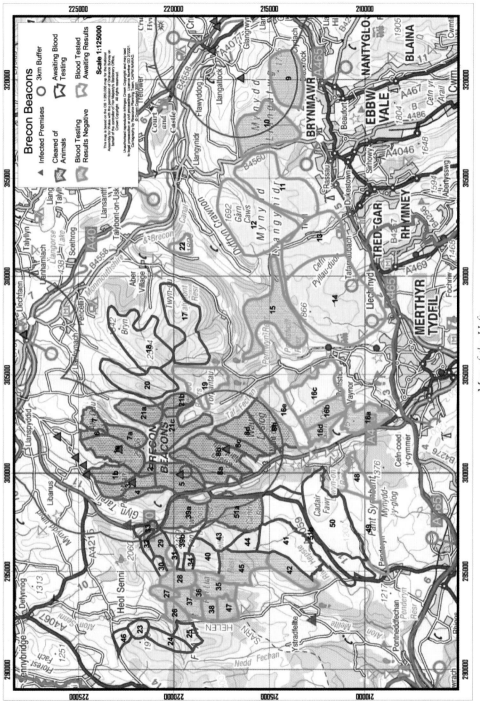

Map of the Hefts

'A survivor'.

So two of the premises, IP 1801 and IP 1806, had been declared infected premises on the basis of just one antibody positive test result. This seemed ridiculous to me. I read on.

'Spread from the Libanus cluster towards the Brecon Beacons'

When I read through paragraph 21, I went clammy cold:

'IP 1779 had further sheep grazing at Cwm Llwch, on premises which were contiguous to the virus positive and seropositive sheep of IP 1789 at Llwyn Bedw and also contiguous to the common grazing area of the Brecon Beacons. The sheep at Cwm Llwch having been exposed to FMD were slaughtered on 12 July 2001. At slaughter, clinical disease was evident in all 140 of a group of rams indicating a heavy weight of infection and progressive, propagating disease at the premises. Of 57 rams sampled virus was isolated from 39 and antibody was demonstrated in 19. Thirteen of the antibody sheep were also virus positive.'

Suddenly I had no case against their decision to cull, and panic started to take over. This information totally threw out every argument against the culls that had gone on. At the end of Scudamore's statement was a map showing numbered areas across the whole of the Brecon Beacons National Park. It was a horrible little map and seemed to me to be a plan for killing. It was supposed to be a reduced version of the large coloured A2 maps that DEFRA had supplied for the hearing, but it was not. There were no infected premises shown on it, and it was titled: Hefts on the Brecon Beacons. I closed the file.

Bryn was furiously making longhand notes of everything that was said. I looked across to Pat and the look on her face was bleak. Matthew had been silent the whole time and I wondered what he was making of it all.

Guy Adams was speaking of the nature of the hefted sheep on the Beacons and explained that they graze on the hillside without enclosure, and know their own territory, which is passed down from generation to generation. 'The risks' he said 'of the virus spreading from one flock of hefted sheep to another is of a much lesser order then intensely farmed animals in bounded fields.' He made the point about the difficulty of reintroducing other flocks once the hefted flock has been culled and cited the remarks made by Edwin Harris to the press, that it could take 20 to 30 years to re-establish flocks on the Brecon Beacons. Judge Burnton said 'Yes' a lot in response to the points raised by Guy and I began to be hopeful that he was starting to be convinced of the argument.

The judge asked what relief was being sought and Guy Adams said that the claim sought a quashing order on the decision to cull 6,000 sheep without testing. Judge Burnton looked puzzled and said that quashing normally means that one 'quashes the legal effects of an administrative act.' Guy Adams then came to a conclusion that a declaration would be best.

'What declaration?' asked Judge Burnton.

'That those decisions were unlawful,' said Guy Adams. It felt as if Guy Adams was being tied up in knots. The judge then said that this would have the consequence that farmers could not lawfully be compensated. Guy Adams was prepared for this one because he said that if the decision was unlawful then the culling would have been a trespass and the Secretary of State would be liable for the value of their sheep in any event. The judge would not be swayed from his conviction that the matter of compensation stood in the way of quashing or a declaration. The farmers agreed to what occurred, he had noted. Of course, I thought. The graziers had been made to sign forms of consent in order to prevent the culling being trespass and illegal. If they had refused to sign the forms then no culling could have taken place.

The issue of compensation remained an unresolved thorn in the side of Guy's argument. The judge considered that it was necessary for the farmers to be interested parties. Guy had pointed out Brian Bowen's witness statement in support of my case but it was obviously insufficient in the eyes of Judge Burnton.

Guy Adams went on to discuss the chronology of the outbreak at Libanus and how when test results were returning as negative the Welsh Assembly had announced a change of policy on 9 August. Sheep were now to be killed before the return of blood test results.

The judge then came out with a statement that I might have found funny if watching a play at a theatre.

He said: 'Well, let us assume that they just guess, they lick a finger, put it in the air, the wind is blowing from the west and they say, right, we will kill them. When they actually test the carcasses they find that their guess was right. Do you say the court in those circumstances should quash the decision to cull?'

'My Lord, I am saying they could have discovered that by a route which would have–'

'I understand that, but I am asking you whether you say in those circumstances the court should quash the decision.'

Guy Adams reminded the judge that he could exercise his discretion to quash and that the decision to cull might well have been unlawful, even if later justified. So far I had not seen any such justification.

There was a return to the issue of who had been making the decisions. The judge said that the defendants were saying there had been no delegation, just agency. Guy Adams pointed out that, whatever had been happening, it had not been a mere operational application of existing DEFRA policy.

The judge felt that Mr Scudamore was saying that one's policy 'develops as one, I was going to say lives and learns, but it is more like kills and learns.'

'Precisely,' Guy Adams said, and went on to say that the chronology suggested that the political influence from the wrong person taking the decisions may well have had an influence on the chronology.

'Your Lordship will recall on 7 August there was a special meeting of the National Assembly for Wales–'

I knew, from the press releases of the Welsh Assembly and from what various graziers had said, that Carwyn Jones had been making decisions that he was not empowered to make, and thousands of people in Wales knew that too. However, was the judge going to be convinced of this? I doubted it.

'There is nothing wrong with people having an influence on decisions provided decisions are made by those to whom Parliament has given the relevant discretion.'

'My Lord, if it was a rubber stamping exercise–'

'That is something else' said the judge, quite severely. He then went on to note that Mr Jones had been claiming 'to be responsible for certain other decisions, on one view, for which he is not the person to pull the trigger or bite the bullet.'

'Or, my Lord, set the policy,'

'Absolutely,' ended Judge Burnton.

Oh, he seemed to be back on our side again, but then that hope faded when he said that the heart of the case was about the substance of the policy and the decisions, rather than who was doing what. The whole point of Guy's argument on this aspect had been to try and show the judge that who was making the decisions had a great bearing on the substance of those decisions. The judge had neatly side stepped that now.

Guy Adams reinforced his point about the graziers being persuaded at a meeting to agree to the culling.

'Are you asking me to infer that this cull took place because, only because, the graziers agreed?'

'Yes, my Lord.' replied Guy Adams.

The judge then suggested a break for lunch, as it was 1.05pm. The hearing would resume at 2.05pm. A court usher called for everyone to stand up and then Judge Burnton left the courtroom.

31

Luncheon Panic

All of us left the courtroom and went into the long corridor. Guy Adams came up to us. He was in a terrible state over the 140 rams full of virus. I told him that I just could not understand it. Nothing had been mentioned in the press or in the list of IPs and Edwin Harris had not mentioned anything about them either. It was a nightmare and I felt Guy's panic rising. He said that he was going to study the papers during lunch and he took off on his own, weighed down by loads of files. Dafydd said that he had brought some sandwiches with him and went off to eat them.

Bryn, Pat, Matthew and I walked down through the hall and out into the sunshine. Several photographers were there. We walked across the busy road and found a sandwich bar. Matthew had a nice egg and cress roll; Pat and myself had some salad rolls. Bryn bought some too and joked about his black eye, the result of playing rugby that weekend. He said that he had to buy another file pad as he had used up the other one. We found a stationer's nearby and after he had bought the pad we walked back into the court hall and found an alcove in which to sit down. Then we all munched the fresh rolls and I began to feel less shaky.

I asked Bryn how he felt things were going. He said that he thought there was a chance that the judge would grant a review but it depended on what happened after lunch. The barristers there on behalf of DEFRA had been virtually silent during the morning proceedings and they were obviously going to try and prevent a review happening. The 140 rams were so troubling. This information had thrown Guy Adams and he did seem to have lost all confidence in the case. I had never trusted DEFRA or the Welsh Assembly on their stance during foot and mouth and I did not trust them now on this one. However, I had no proof that it was a lie.

The hour passed too quickly and it was soon time to return to the courtroom. We went up the short flight of steps and into the dark corridor again. Guy Adams was already there and looked as if he had been there all the time, studying the documents. He smiled but I could tell that he felt his whole argument had fallen apart. Dafydd came to join us and we went back into the courtroom to wait for the judge.

32

The Afternoon Judgment

Afternoon sunshine was streaming in through the high windows and the large clock on the wall seemed to be emphasised. In a few hours time the fate of the sheep would have been decided. I would rather have been sitting in a dentist's waiting room preparing to have all my teeth removed. The court usher called for everyone to stand. The judge returned and resumed his place.

Guy Adams stood up and resumed his argument. He returned to how the decision to cull could be challenged and how there had been the opportunity to test before slaughter at all stages. Judge Burton interrupted and said that the only remedy would seem to be either to quash or a declaration of unlawfulness. Guy Adams agreed. The fact that the sheep had already been culled seemed to stand in the way of a declaration for some reason. The judge said that his current view was that the only ground on which to seek relief was that the minister's action had been perverse, irrational. There then followed a fairly lengthy discussion between Guy Adams and the judge on the issue of irrationality and mention was made again of the opportunity for re-testing.

'If one is bringing animals in and penning them for ten days,' said Guy, 'then there is an opportunity to re-test.'

'Clearly,' said Judge Burnton.

Judge Burnton asked Guy Adams which decision he considered irrational; the order to cull at the end of July or the cull on 6 August? Guy Adams said that he did not have all the information on the testing and it might be that there was no active infection anywhere. No test results for virus had been produced by DEFRA and the only inference that Guy Adams could draw from this was that no virus had been found. Good, he was ignoring the 140 rams bit. He said that the lack of test results for virus suggested that the disease had been present several months ago and had left a number of antibody positive sheep, and that there was no evidence of any spread at all.

The judge concluded from these remarks that Guy Adams found both decisions irrational. Guy Adams then returned to the issue of the injunction and the senior counsel for DEFRA said that he thought his 'friend was abandoning this.' Poor Guy, he seemed caught up between the smirks of the judge and the other barristers. I was shocked at their behaviour, which seemed to border on contempt. It felt to me as if both the judge and the other barristers found my case to be a cause for ridicule and mirth. I wanted to stand up and shout at them and tell them how rude they were being, but all I could do was to glare at them in silence. Dafydd was sighing behind me and Pat was looking furious. I was not the only one to be angry at the behaviour in court. It was very unprofessional and I felt sorry for Guy. He was trying his best to present the truth as clearly as possible but it was becoming increasingly plain from the expressions being passed between the judge and the other barristers that his argument was falling on stony ground. This judge seemed to be siding with the barristers from DEFRA and the Assembly and when the hearing had finished Dafydd and Pat told me that they both held the same opinion.

Guy Adams then came to the other interim application, which was for further information to be given as to what tests had been carried out and what the results were. He pointed out that this information had been requested for about ten days. The judge said that depended on permission being given and Guy Adams had come to the end of his submission.

The Assembly barrister launched into his attack on the case and told Judge Burnton that the National Assembly was deeply concerned and sympathetic to the position the farmers found themselves in. I wanted to laugh out loud. Here was Carwyn Jones holding meetings and apparently forcing graziers to sign consent forms, and all of a sudden the Assembly was concerned. What a sick joke and blatant lie. The Welsh barrister then went on to say that it was DEFRA and not the Assembly, that had been taking the decisions. He produced various authorities and agency agreements. Why had Guy Adams not checked this? Or were these more lies? My case was being torn apart.

He ended his submission and the senior barrister for DEFRA began. He started by saying that the Secretary of State shared the concern of the National Assembly for Wales about the sheep on the Beacons. Yes, shared the concern of how to get rid of the poor sheep as quickly as possible I thought. These clever tongues were lying and cheating and shredding my case and there was nothing I could do to stop it happening. The DEFRA barrister smartly stepped his way through the arguments put forward by the judge in relation to the illegitimacy of considering the attitude of the graziers.

'One can see the reason why one needed consent; the logistical problems.'

Oh very clever. Don't forget that without consent the culls could not have taken place lawfully.

The counsel for DEFRA went on to the test results and came to heft 8, an area of hillside to the south of the central peaks, from where thousands of sheep had been culled on the basis of five sheep having tested positive for antibodies according to Edwin Harris. The barrister went over the results of heft 8 in detail and the judge became confused and so the barrister went through them a second time. The important aspect of these results was that apparently there had been 1 VNT inconclusive on the first test. The judge then put him very much on the spot and the barrister coloured a deep red, including his ears. Judge Burnton asked how you could have an inconclusive VNT.

The barrister then had to turn to the man with the pock marked face seated directly in front of him. They had a brief exchange of conversation and the barrister said:

'I do not know if your Lordship heard that, both are taken on a range and effectively, so far as an ELISA test is concerned, anything between 40 and 70 per cent is considered to be inconclusive.'

He then went on to say that the slaughter on heft 8 was not on the basis of tests. 'It was on the basis that it was contiguous to heft 5. That was the reason it was carried out.'

But these poor animals had been penned for days on that hillside awaiting test results. From what this red-faced barrister was saying, it didn't matter what the results were; they were already dead by being contiguous to heft 5, where they had only found antibodies in any case.

The sheep on heft 8 had been sampled on 27 July, with overall results being 'inconclusive', according to Mr Scudamore's witness statement. 'Due to the known links with the disease and contiguity with heft 5b, the sheep were slaughtered on 4 August 2001 with the agreement of the owner and re-bled.' Mr Scudamore's statement then went on to say that the 'subsequent tests confirmed the epidemiological predictions: the tests gave an overall result of positive, indicating that the disease had developed within the flock over the period between the first and second tests.' In fact the opposite was the case. The test results were 'overall negative' according to the laboratory report, which I only discovered in 2004.

The graziers had agreed to the pre-emptive cull of some 6,000 sheep from contiguous hefts on 9 August 2001, the same day as the second set of test results for heft 8 had returned. These results had shown that there was no spread of disease whatsoever and had the graziers known the truth about heft 8 they would have realised that a pre-emptive cull was completely unnecessary and unwarranted.

Official documents, also discovered in 2004, show that the control policy of the National Assembly for Wales Agricultural Division, (NAWAD), had been applied to heft 8. In other words, the Welsh Assembly had been responsible for ordering the slaughter of around two thousand healthy hefted sheep, knowing that the test results were negative.

Bryn was still furiously scribbling away and I thought how tired his hand must be. The stenographer sitting at the front was tapping away on her machine, but Bryn's task was much harder, without the ease of shorthand. When I later compared Bryn's notes of the judgment with the formal copy from Smith Bernal, the official transcribers, they were practically identical.

The next pieces of discussion between the barrister for DEFRA and the judge still arouse such anger in me that I do not know quite where to put it. The judge asked about the policy to 'pen and test' and how it had come to be changed to 'kill before testing'. The barrister told him that the policy had not worked. Judge Burnton said that it was not very clear to him why it was thought it did not work. The barrister then said,

'Well, it was not—'

Judge Burnton then cut in and said, 'It clearly did not work because the disease spread'.

'Yes', crowed the grinning barrister.

The two men sitting at the front, a few feet directly in front of the judge, have troubled me since. The one was the pock marked man, to whom the barrister for DEFRA turned for information on testing. The other man was a little man with dark hair and dark spectacles. They appeared to me to be keeping an eye on the judge. Now suddenly, from being unclear as to why the penning and testing was not working, the judge had arrived at the answer in seconds, even saving the DEFRA barrister from trying to answer the question himself.

I knew my case had failed as soon as the judge said that ' as far as the past is concerned, I have already indicated, it seems to me, it would be quite wrong for a case to go forward which might upset those decisions and their consequences.'

The future was then spoken of and my legal standing. The DEFRA barrister told the judge that what he didn't have before him, was 'a grazier who has sheep on hefts 19 and 20.'

'20, did you say, or 19?' asked Judge Burnton.

'20,19,18, and 17. Those were next,' replied the barrister

'Has 16..?' Judge Burnton was stopped short.

'No 16 has also not been culled, but 20...'.

'I can see that they may be sleeping easier because they do not have a risk of infection on their doorstop,' ended the judge. Oh, how I wish I had known then that my ten sheep grazed on heft 17.

Guy Adams rose to his feet to make his final closing remarks. He told the court that 'we do not have a complete picture and cannot put together the jigsaw puzzle as to whether or not this disease was historic or active. Your Lordship will note the complete lack of any evidence of active disease on the hefts. If there had been a single positive probang result on any of the sheep that had been slaughtered on the Brecon Beacons, then I have absolutely no doubt that my learned friend would have been relying strongly on that before your Lordship. It is the policy of DEFRA to take probang tests on slaughter to see whether there is any active infection. The only conclusion your Lordship could draw is all these sheep were slaughtered without having any infectivity in the hills.' He sat down.

Guy Adams could not have made a clearer case for the need for a judicial review but it was a forgone conclusion that Mr Justice Stanley Burnton was going to refuse permission. You could see it in his eyes and in his glances towards the other barristers. There was no way that this judge would rule in my favour.

He launched into his summing up and judgment, and finally he was saying the dreaded words; 'Therefore permission is refused.'

It felt as if a noose was being placed round my neck. The horrible little map of all the heft areas lay open again in front of me, and it took on the appearance of a map of doom. The courtroom became darker as the rays of the afternoon sun grew dim and I looked at the clock. The fate of the sheep had now been sealed and I felt as if I had totally failed them. How I hated this courtroom and the judge.

The barristers rose to their feet and started demanding their costs. Guy Adams told the judge that he had complete discretion as to whether to award them any costs or not, but Judge Burnton was not listening. He agreed to award their costs, to be decided at a later date. The amounts being demanded were £4,000 for the Assembly and £21,000 for DEFRA. I had become numb by this time and these amounts of money meant nothing compared to what was to happen to the sheep. I didn't care and just wanted to go home. I dared not imagine what Matthew was thinking or feeling.

As we left the courtroom a woman came up to me and said she was a reporter from the Daily Mail. I had noticed her sitting at the front of the courtroom making notes throughout the hearing. She asked me a few questions about what I thought of the outcome and what my intentions were. I told her that I was dismayed and that I intended to appeal. We walked out into the corridor. Guy Adams came up and said that he was sorry he had been unable to obtain permission. I told him that I wanted to appeal; there seemed little alternative and even if there had not been the matter of thousands of pounds in costs I would have wished to appeal for the sake of the sheep. He made it clear that he felt this stood very little chance of success but that he was willing to try.

Dafydd Morris had left just after the judge had finished his final speech. He had whispered how disgusted he was and that he would be in contact. Pat, Bryn, Matthew and I walked back out of the court and into the late afternoon brightness. There was still a group of reporters and cameramen outside but Bryn told me not to say anything to them. I decided that I wanted to though and agreed to speak with the reporter from the Shropshire Star, who had been in the courtroom. Amongst other things, I told him that I had done as much as I could and that it was now up to the farmers. I only found out later from Glyn that my comments to the reporter were shown on BBC Wales 6 o'clock news that evening. Roy Miller, the farmer from near Welshpool, who had been involved with Unity, had apparently been interviewed and he had said that now the only way forward was a public inquiry.

I thought about Mr Justice Stanley Burnton's summing up, and how, in his consideration, my case stood 'no real prospect of success.' Well, he had certainly made sure of that.

33

Journey Home

We said farewell to Bryn and Guy as they went to catch a taxi to the station. Then Pat asked if we wanted to go and have a drink. Oh yes indeed. All three of us were weary and in need of some refreshment. We walked over the road and I saw the Wig and Pen. They did not allow children though and so we found a bar nearby. Pat got us some drinks and I went off to the Ladies. I felt quite sick but glad that the ordeal was over. Pat and Matthew had found a table near a window and we sat and tried to console each other. Pat had no good words to say about the judge and neither had Matthew. All of us felt that he had been bought off. She had made notes too and went over them, adding bits that she had not had time to write.

I rang Glyn from a phone box outside, before we caught the bus to Victoria Station. He was devastated at the news. Then I remembered my camera still in the little shop, so it was a dash back to pick that up. The bus came and we clambered up to the top deck. I was still trying to make sense of the day's events and numbness was beginning to turn to anger. The mobile rang and it was a reporter; I can't recall who or which paper. I told her that I felt totally fed up but that I intended to appeal. The bus reached Victoria and we clambered back down the spiral stairway. Pat had come down by coach and we walked to the coach station to see her off. After a big hug she disappeared amongst the crowds and Matthew and I walked back to Warwick Way to pick up the luggage left at the hotel. It was a beautiful summer's afternoon, almost evening by now, and the window boxes with their bright flowers nearly brightened me up. A huge aeroplane flew low overhead, presumably from Heathrow. People were starting to pack up their wares from the pavements outside their shops and wine bars were beginning to look busy.

We caught a bus to Euston station. Matthew wanted to sit upstairs again but I persuaded him to stay down. The mobile rang. It was Andrew Forgrave, the farming editor of the Daily Post. He wanted to know what had happened and was very disappointed at the outcome and aghast when I mentioned the potential amount of costs awarded against me. The bus reached Euston and I rang off. Soon we were on the train home and it was a very despondent journey for me. It all felt like complete failure. Guy Adams had tried his best and he could not really have done any more. He was not a magician and he had given as good a performance as he could in the face of contemptuous ridicule. I settled down to read through DEFRA's evidence and Matthew became lost in his book.

Darkness started to fall as we neared Shrewsbury. Glyn was waiting on the platform and he gave us both a hug. He told us of the news reports as we drove home. Matthew was so happy to be tucked up on the back seat. I felt incredibly wound up and so tired that I felt like crying. We told him about what had happened in court and how the judge had laughed with the other barristers. He agreed with me on the appeal aspect and as we drove along the dark lanes home, hope began to mingle with the disappointment.

It was wonderful to be back home. Several people had rung during the day and Glyn showed me the list. A woman called Beatrice from Country Life, had phoned, and various reporters from the press and television. The case had failed and I did not expect that they would be contacting me further.

34

Media Post-Mortem

When I woke up the next morning I felt like lead. The disappointment hit me and I didn't want to get up. Glyn had gone to buy some newspapers before going to work and he brought them home. There we were in the Daily Telegraph with the bad news. I looked white-haired in the photo and Matthew looked very disappointed. A friend who lived in Portsmouth, and who has since died, told me that I looked as if I'd just come out of prison! The Times had a piece on it and the photo echoed the distress I had felt after the hearing. The Western Mail had a front-page piece on it and I was heartened at the supportive publicity in the face of failure. Glyn went off to work and I tried to feel positive for Matthew.

As soon as I came downstairs the phone rang. It was a reporter from BBC Radio Shropshire. He had heard the outcome and asked if I would give an interview for the morning programme. I was glad to spill the beans and have the opportunity of letting people know what had happened in court the previous day. Then before I'd had time to turn round and get us breakfast the phone rang again. This time it was BBC Wales, wanting an interview. I was astonished, as I had assumed no one would wish to talk with someone who had failed in their mission. Penny Roberts, the chief reporter, arranged to come up later that day to do an interview. Goodness, I thought, I was going to have to get myself together. I had been expecting a day of silence and the opposite was happening.

A listener to the programme on Radio Shropshire phoned. He was very sympathetic and said he had had experience of the judiciary acting like this. It was good to talk about the case to someone fairly local because the silence of our village had got me down of late. The people with whom I had been discussing the case had tended to be reporters and solicitors and the support of the media meant a great deal. The man wished me the best of luck and rang off. Penny Roberts had said she would aim to get here by 1 o'clock, so I had to start getting my skates on if I was to be presentable. I got us breakfast, very late, and then ran baths for us.

Then I took out DEFRA's evidence again and started going through the witness statements and their chronology, put in during the hearing. Oh yes, Judge Burnton had allowed this, but had not allowed evidence from me about Pirbright's statement of being able to test for virus within 4 hours. The DEFRA barrister had said that it would be 'hotly disputed' and the evidence was not allowed in any case. One rule for the Government and one rule for the individual; this was meant to be a democracy? Before I made the application I had held some faith with the impartiality of the judiciary but ever since 2001 that faith has crumbled, particularly after the appeal hearing that was to follow in January 2002.

The morning disappeared quickly and 1pm was fast approaching. I was becoming nervous but I wanted to get across the main points in the interview and the fact that DEFRA's chronology was proof that so many of the test results had come back negative. No wonder they had not wanted to put that in prior to the hearing. I made some sandwiches for Matthew and myself, and then we saw a large vehicle out by the gate. I went to shut the dogs in the conservatory, because they tend to overwhelm anyone who comes to Laurels Cottage. We have five of them, of all sorts, and they are too friendly really, and let loose would cause visitors to leave covered in muddy paw shapes.

A tall, slim lady came to meet me at the gate. She was very friendly and at once made me at ease. It was a good job I had shut the dogs in because she was wearing a cream trouser suit. The cameraman was coming from Wrexham way and he arrived just after she had introduced herself as Penny Roberts. They both came into our cluttered cottage and Penny took charge. She told the cameraman what type of shots she was after and then my job was to clear our kitchen table of the piles of newspapers and paraphernalia. Then, as the cameraman shone the very bright light on me, I went over what had happened so far and gave details of the hearing. Penny was very interested in DEFRA's chronology and the camera homed in on it. That evening the news report showed this chronology with all the negative test results and many people rang me about this after watching the programme.

Penny wanted shots here, there and everywhere. She got shots of me at the computer, of Matthew at the table writing out a plan of attack for the appeal, and then shots of the garden. By the time we reached the garden shots they had been here nearly two hours and I had been amazed at the detail of all the procedure for the camerawork and interviewing. Shots were repeated, as was conversation, until Penny felt that it was how she wanted it. As we stood chatting on the lawn she realised that she knew the cameraman but had not seen him for many years. They talked about when they had last met and Penny said that only recently she had been looking at some photos of their meeting. Then she put on some make-up and stood in front of our cottage to give her introduction for the news item. Matthew was fascinated and enjoyed them being here. After the trauma of the hearing it was nice to have something positive coming out of it.

Penny then said she must dash back to Cardiff and the cameraman was heading north. She was concerned about my intentions to take the case as far as possible, including the European Court of Human Rights, but was so supportive that I felt better already. The judge's verdict was disappearing into the distant past already.

35

Preparations for Appeal

On Thursday morning I realised that I had not heard from Mr Wilkins since the hearing. I had been very disappointed that he had been unable to be at the hearing. He had told me that he had to be at a meeting that day for business clients of Dolmans, and even though he had apologised for not being able to come down to London, I felt let down. Bryn had been brilliant though and had supported me such a lot. At every move he had been there to guide me and I was very impressed; nothing had seemed too much trouble for him. The other thing was that with the hourly rate for a solicitor being some £125, then perhaps it was just as well that Mr Wilkins had stayed behind to look after his corporate clients!

Anyway, Mr Wilkins rang later that morning and practically told me off for being unavailable on the Wednesday. He said that he had tried several times to contact me but that the phone was engaged all the time. Unfortunately, I became slightly heated at him.

The appeal had to be at the court within seven days, he was telling me. It was already Thursday and there was also Bank Holiday coming up, so time was very short. He was very agitated. I told him how dismayed I had been at the behaviour of the judge and the barristers for DEFRA. If he had been there he would have seen it too.

Mr Wilkins said that the letter relating to the costs had to be at the court by Friday 24 August, tomorrow, and this was the cause of his agitation. He had received DEFRA's submission and had tried to argue for their requested costs to be reduced radically. The Assembly's costs seemed fairly reasonable he felt. I didn't feel any of the costs were reasonable or just. I had been refused a judicial review and many months later I discovered that the general rule is that costs are not awarded against a claimant at the permission stage. I wish that Mr Wilkins had known of this rule. He was also going to have to hire a London agent, to take the application forms into the Court of Appeal, he said. The deadline was Tuesday 28 August and the forms would have to be with the agent by the following day. We agreed the terms of the appeal and he said that he would ask Guy to draft it. Then the form was faxed through for me to sign and the week came to an end.

For the first time in ages I felt able to relax a little, even though we did not know what was going to happen to all the remaining thousands of sheep on the Beacons. DEFRA had stated to the court that no more culling was planned and this statement had to provide us with sufficient comfort for the time being. Bank Holiday Monday arrived and we had a quiet day. Tuesday arrived and all the paperwork had gone to London by courier. Wednesday, 29 August came and with it a phone call from Jon Townsley to Mr Wilkins, asking if I was taking the case to appeal. If they were not planning more culling then why were they so interested in whether or not it was going to appeal? I do believe, the more I have thought it through, that had I not taken the case onwards, then the culling would have started up again. However, with the eyes of the law still potentially on them, they would not dare further illegal coercion and killing.

The agent duly delivered the forms and as I later found out from the invoices, duly charged over £400 for this. The agent's office is just round the corner from the court office and £400 was a nice amount for this little job, which must have taken no more than half-hour to complete.

It then transpired that Mr Justice Stanley Burnton had gone on holiday until October and had left before making a decision on the costs issue. Maybe the old bird was on my side slightly more than I had thought.

To our amazement the post became a deluge of donations and wonderful letters of encouragement. Each day more and more poured in, until the fund contained over £10,000. I felt humbled at the faith of people in my case; I had failed at the first hurdle but they still believed in the case. This support made me even more determined to carry on.

The testing of the remaining flocks in the Brecon Beacons National Park continued through early September. My ten sheep on heft 17 were penned and tested a couple of weeks after the hearing and it was a fairly anxious time. I had phoned Mr and Mrs Williams, who had 'sold' me the ten sheep, to check how things were going and they were both very positive. They had a large flock and my ten sheep were anonymous amongst them. Mrs Williams told me that the sheep were being held in a pen. The mention of pens caused me alarm but she told me not to worry, as their sheep needed shearing. Apparently sheep on other hefts were being penned and tested and then released, unless the owners wished to shear them.

When I phoned on 11 September Mr Williams had good news. The results had been negative. He said that he felt the authorities were just 'going through the motions' and no more positive results would be found. He was right. All the remaining thousands of sheep on the Brecon Beacons received the all clear and we breathed a sigh of relief.

Many months later I came across some information, which showed that negative test results had been applied to several hefts that had in fact not been tested. (Appendix 1, page 235). It did seem that the authorities had abandoned their quest to find any further foot and mouth disease in the sheep of the Brecon Beacons.

36

'Angels of Death'

Mr Wilkins made arrangements for a meeting with Guy Adams at his Chambers in Bristol. It was planned for 19 September. So then I got busy examining Mr Scudamore's witness statement, in preparation for the meeting. When I had come home from London after the hearing I had told Glyn and Matthew that I felt there was a lie in the statement. Looking back I should have spotted it immediately but it took several weeks until the truth and the lie were uncovered.

I received an unexpected phone call during the afternoon of 31 August. It was the slaughter man, from Hay-on-Wye. He told me that he was keeping to his promise of letting me know of any plans for more culls. I grabbed a piece of paper. He went through the areas that were planned. They plan to cull sheep, he said, from the northern edge of the Brecon Beacons up through the Cambrian Mountains, on to Bala, then Hiraethog, and then into Snowdonia. There were also plans for mass culls in other areas of the Brecon Beacons.

'They've had the one side and the other will be next.'

I asked him when the plans were due to start but he couldn't tell me that he said, because he didn't know for sure. Apparently a further two million sheep in Wales were ear-marked to be killed. They were seven weeks behind schedule, he said. I wondered what schedule. He stayed on the phone for quite some time and spoke of the days when he used to go up onto the Black Mountains as a child to pick wimberries, and how the shepherding of the sheep on the mountains was so much better then. How times had changed, he said. He sounded wistful. I asked him if they had known the sheep back in June would be killed prior to test results. Oh yes, he said, they knew. The test results had nothing to do with the decision; the plans had already been made.

He then said that he'd better go, as it was time for his tea. I asked him if he would mind if I rang him again, and he said that would be fine and that we'd have to meet one day, in better times. Our meeting has not come about, and probably I shall never see him face to face. I did ring him later in the autumn to check if anything else was planned and it wasn't, as far as he knew, thank God. He told me that he'd not been well and was soon due to retire, and I gained the impression that he would be very glad to retire away from actions that even he found distasteful and not in keeping with the country way of life.

On 3 September a map of the Brecon Beacons appeared with a press release on the web site of the Welsh Assembly. The map showed the hefts and which hefts had been cleared of sheep and which were awaiting testing or test results. It was so brightly coloured and the areas coloured in red seemed to speak of the blood that had been spilt on those mountains. I hated the map, but I felt it was very significant. Again, it was several months until I discovered the true significance of the map.

I thought of what the slaughter man had told me. That evening I wrote out a letter for Carwyn Jones, and listed the areas that the man had told me were planned for culling. I sent copies to Tony Edwards, Lembit Opik, our MP, and Bob Parry, the Chairman of the FUW. The Cabinet Office of the Welsh Assembly sent an acknowledgement slip, but not a reply, and I never received a response from the other people. The culls never took place, thanks to the slaughter man. Dafydd Morris rang a few weeks later and said he had seen machinery up in Snowdonia, and that it had been taken away. That gladdened our hearts.

On 7 September Bonnie Durrance arrived. She is from California and was making a film about Foot and Mouth, entitled 'Nobody Talks About It.' It was a very apt title I thought because there was a very definite wall of silence about the whole thing. She had phoned me back in August, when she had read the newspaper reports, and said she would like to include our tale in her film.

It felt as if we had known Bonnie for a long time. She did a bit of filming here at home and then we went off down to the Brecon Beacons after lunch. It was a beautiful early autumn afternoon and soon the Black Mountains were in sight. Bonnie parked her car at the side of the road and

I pointed out Llangoed Hall, at Llyswen, the hotel where, according to Brian Bowen, there had been a meeting in late July/early August. The meeting had been between DEFRA, the State Veterinary Service and the Welsh Assembly. A person known to Brian Bowen worked for the Welsh Assembly and had seen details of the meeting, which apparently had the title of 'Preparations for plans of a mass cull of sheep on the southern areas of the Brecon Beacons.' It sounded as if it was akin to the meetings held by the Nazis for their plans on the extermination of the Jews. No minutes were available and the person was too scared to give out any further information, which was a great pity.

We carried on and a short while later arrived at the northern edge of the Brecon Beacons National Park. There is something very special about the Brecon Beacons; they have a presence that makes one feel very humbled. We reached the city of Brecon, a pretty place made miniature by the towering mountains, which rise up a handful of miles away. I thought of the children of the area who would have seen the poor sheep being gathered off those high slopes. We drove on down the A470 towards Libanus. The little village felt sad as we drove through it. A few miles further on down the road we found a lay-by. Bonnie took out her cameras and asked me to point out exactly where we were in the Park. In an enclosed field next to the main road was a small flock of sheep, nibbling away quietly. This field was so near to where the culls had taken place that it was a miracle that these sheep had survived. I wondered if they had been forgotten in the haste of the slaughter. Whatever the reason, we were very glad the see them. Matthew went to have a closer look at them.

The slopes of the mountains behind were empty and the valley floor, which runs between the slopes and the A470, was devoid of livestock except for a couple of horses. This was the valley where thousands of sheep had been killed in June, and I tried to put place names to the farmsteads below. This was the first time that I had been near the Beacons since March that year, and it was a relief in a way, to at last return to the place that had occupied my thoughts and dreams, and nightmares, of recent months. Bonnie's filming was completed, and waving goodbye to the munching sheep, we drove on.

We took Bonnie to meet Mr Gatehouse in late afternoon. I hadn't visited him before and it proved a bit difficult to find his farmhouse, which is tucked away up a lane not far from Llangorse Lake, a large natural lake in the National Park. We eventually found the farm and loads of black and white kittens came to meet us from the yard behind the farm- house. We went to one of the doors and called out. A young teenage girl came to see who was there and smiled. She was one of Mr Gatehouse's daughters. Mrs Gatehouse appeared. They were very welcoming and invited us in. Mr Gatehouse wouldn't be long; he was out in the fields with his son. He arrived back shortly and his wife, Anne, went to make us some tea. We went into the sitting room and Bonnie was very interested in listening to what Mr Gatehouse had to tell her. He is a mine of information and he revelled in Bonnie's attention.

After tea and cakes, Mr Gatehouse asked if we'd like to go up to the top of Llangorse Hill and have a fine view of the lake. We all piled into his old landrover. I sat inside and Matthew, Bonnie and Mr Gatehouse's daughter, Eluned, climbed into the open back. The sun was starting to become low in the sky as the landrover lurched its way up Llangorse Hill and the view became more and more incredible. Llangorse Lake stretched out across the valley floor like a huge mirror, reflecting the orange sky. Mr Gatehouse noticed one of his sheep was caught in a hedge and stopped the landrover to go and pull her out. It was wonderful to see sheep again. All the fields near us had been empty for such a long time. In through another hedge and we had reached the top of the hill. We climbed out.

Bonnie asked Mr Gatehouse if he minded being interviewed. His smile said it all, and she set up her tripod and video camera on the grassy slope. As he proudly talked to Bonnie in the setting sun Eluned chatted with Matthew and I. She told us how she had watched the 'angels of death' in their white suits across the valley that summer. From the top of the hill you can see across the whole of the eastern and central parts of the Brecon Beacons and she would have had to witness those 'angels of death' go about their devilish business. She told us in a very matter of fact way, but her words also held a great anger at what had happened to the animals. I felt angry for her. She wants to follow in her Dad's footsteps and become a farmer; may she never have to witness such evil events again in her lifetime.

Darkness was falling when we returned to Mr Gatehouse's cottage. We were a long way from home and afternoon had imperceptibly turned to 9.30pm. I rang Glyn to tell him we'd be home later than expected and then we went in search of a pub for supper. Everywhere was closing or had finished serving food. 10 pm and Wales had closed! We did find a fish and chip place in Brecon, and then travelled on, finally arriving home gone midnight.

Bonnie was introduced to Glyn and then we sorted out the sofa bed for her. I gave her Bryn's copy of the judgment to have a look at and we went off to bed. The next morning was lovely and full of sunshine. Bonnie had had a relatively peaceful night amongst the cats apparently, which was good or maybe she was being generous! She wanted to take photos of us before she left. Bobby, our Alsatian, fell in love with her and wanted go off with her. The feeling was mutual it seemed! There was to be a meeting sponsored by Compassion in World Farming in Bristol on 15 September, and Bonnie was hoping to be there too, so we said farewell until then, and she drove off.

37

Bristol Meetings

The days flew past and soon 15 September arrived. We almost didn't make it to the CIWF meeting, as there were problems with the trains. Mr Gatehouse was going down to it, and had arranged to have a lift with another farmer. I phoned him that morning to say that I didn't think I'd be there, as the trains were haphazard and I was worried we'd not get home. He wanted me to get there and said that it would be a shame if I missed to meet Professor Brown at last. It was a meeting which had primarily been organised for vets and Professor Brown and a couple of other very well known FMD experts were going to be there too; Dr Paul Sutmoller, and Dr Simon Barteling. Mr Gatehouse said that I must get there, so I agreed to risk the trains. We made it just in time for the meeting and saw Christopher Stockdale on the way in. He had been so helpful earlier in the spring, but ever since his involvement with the National Foot and Mouth Group he had seemed to become increasingly critical of my legal action. We exchanged a few words, then went inside.

There were several faces I recognised amongst the chatting groups in the foyer. Alicia Eykyn was there of course, as she had organised the meeting. Bonnie was there talking with a couple who turned out to be Alan and Rosie Beat, the smallholders from Devon. We went up to say hello and Bonnie gave us a hug. She had tears in her eyes as we spoke of the terrible happening over the World Trade Centre on 11 September. I saw that Mr Gatehouse had arrived; he was busily chatting to a group of folk. Then Pat came up to say hello. Someone then called to ask everyone to go into the auditorium.

Pat came to sit with Matthew and myself. I saw Michaela sitting across the aisle, and Mr Gatehouse was sat over there also, looking very keen. A group of people, including Alicia, came down the aisle, and one of them said something in a voice I immediately recognised as Professor Brown's. I stood up without thinking and called out to him, 'Professor Fred!' He turned round and realised it was me. We shook hands and he gave a big smile. So at last I had met him after the many telephone conversations we had had since April. He was almost as I had imagined him to be; not very tall, wearing spectacles, sprightly, with a kind, quietly determined face. Professor Brown went to sit at the front and then Joyce D'Silva opened the meeting.

It was all very interesting and each of the experts gave a talk of around half an hour. Professor Brown had such a vast knowledge of the FMD virus. He had worked on the virus since 1955; it was he who had discovered its structure. What a tragic waste that the Government ignored his offer of help over FMD in 2001.

There was a short break and I went down to the front to have a few words with Professor Brown and introduced Matthew to him. He was such a pleasant, down to earth person, with no airs and graces, even though the considered world authority on FMD. He said that it was very difficult to understand all the information that had been sent to him by Mr Wilkins; 'like trying to find your way through the desert,' he said. I said how grateful I was for him helping with my case, and then went off for a cup of tea. We bumped into Julian Heath, the vet from Somerset. He had been in the wars with DEFRA legally, whilst attempting to obtain some sort of justice over pay when he had refused to keep on working for them. The outcome did not sound to have been a good one for him and he had come off the worse in financial terms. It always seemed to me as if he lived on some other plane; after that he did seem to take off on his cloud and I didn't hear from him again.

We then returned to the auditorium for the last part of the meeting. Members of the audience were given the opportunity to ask questions. I listened and took notes, and Pat did likewise. Professor Brown then mentioned the 159 sheep that had been penned for 14 days on the Beacons in June, and how after 14 days the same one antibody had been present. This information had been of great significance to him, and he now cited it as evidence that sheep with FMD antibodies are not infectious. He said that someone called Janet Hughes had provided him with the information and asked if I was still there. I raised my hand and a white-haired man sitting immediately in front of me turned round to ask me if it really was true about the 159 sheep. Yes it was, I told him. He looked astonished. Someone later told me that he was a senior vet from DEFRA, who had come along to check on the meeting.

The end of the meeting came and I went to say goodbye to Professor Brown. There was a large crowd of people gathered at the front trying to get the chance to ask each of the experts some more questions individually and so I just shook hands with Professor Fred and said farewell. I was so glad to have met him. Michaela offered us a lift home, which meant that we didn't have to be at the mercy of the railways. As we were leaving, Alicia was dashing around the foyer speaking of meal bookings. Professor Brown would be there of course. I later learnt that she had made a group booking for several members of the National Foot and Mouth Group. Oh well, I thought, never mind, at least I had met Professor Brown.

On the way home Michaela and I had an intense discussion about events of 2001 since our trip to the NFU on 3 April. I had not seen her much since then, even though she only lives a few miles away and it was good to catch up. She had grown very cynical and felt there was little that could be done to prevent the demise of farming, as we know it. Her sheep were okay, except that she had lost one lamb, due to a liver problem. We went astray with directions in the dark and ended up arriving home gone midnight.

It was only 4 days until our meeting with Guy Adams in Bristol. We seemed destined to keep returning to that city. I had booked a room at the Westbury Park Hotel, situated just outside Bristol City Centre. We'd decided to stay there the night and then go on to Portsmouth for a few days, as we do most years. We said our goodbyes to our dogs and cats, and caught the late morning train from Ludlow. Glyn waved us off and crossed his fingers as he stood on the platform. A few hours later and we had arrived in Bristol. We had a fair amount of luggage, as well as all the documents needed for the meeting, and I hauled the bags onto the bus for the city centre.

Guy Adams' Chambers are situated just off the main street of the City Centre. The building is at the end of a narrow street, lined with several interesting shops and smart looking restaurants. As we neared the end of the street where it turns into the part where the Chambers lie, lighted torches flared into view along the walls of the buildings. The Brecon Beacons web site is illustrated with such torches, and it seemed most odd for these torches to be sited outside the very spot where I was going to seek legal help.

'Take nothing but photographs, kill nothing but time, leave nothing but footprints.' Why had they not taken heed of this, the motto of the Brecon Beacons National Park?

The torches glowed and flared as we walked around and on to St John's Chambers. The entrance was in a narrow corridor between the old buildings. We walked up the stairway and saw the notice for the Chambers. I felt that these smart barristers would look strangely at us with all our bags. The receptionist told us she would let Guy Adams know we had arrived and told us to wait across the way in the waiting room. As we sat down Mr Wilkins and Bryn arrived. Guy Adams came to meet us soon after and led us off to his room. He then asked Bryn to take Matthew out, as he needed to ask me a few questions. I was puzzled.

Mr Wilkins and Guy Adams had a quiet word with one another and I began to feel very on edge indeed. A few moments later I was almost in tears, as Guy Adams started interrogating me about the savings that I had used on the case. What ruddy business was it of theirs I wanted to ask? Mr Wilkins watched quietly over his spectacles. Guy Adams had been told of a press report in the Telegraph about my having used up trust funds that were for Matthew. But hadn't this already been sorted out? Mr Wilkins had phoned me the previous day because Guy Adams was apparently concerned about the money used on the case. I had faxed through a letter explaining that we had used savings that I had intended to be for Matthew, but that they were not savings in any formal Trust.

The problem had arisen as a result of a woman from the press phoning the day after the hearing. She had been very pleasant and had asked me about the savings used to pay for the case. I had told her they were savings put by primarily for Matthew and then she had spoken with Matthew. He had said he would rather have the sheep than have money for a car. The next day an article had appeared in 'The Western Mail' and unknown to me in national papers also, and I was extremely annoyed about it. The article had stated that Matthew had given up his savings for the case and that they had been held in Trust. Sue Goddard, the reporter from the Western Mail, had phoned up and she mentioned the article. She had been away and she told me that she would not have written such things unless I had been fully informed and the facts checked. I had very stupidly been caught off guard and the reporter had used what I had said in such a way as to make a headline story. That put me off reporters for a while.

I began to feel very defensive. I explained to Guy Adams and Mr Wilkins that the money had come from our general long-term savings, which I had intended to be used for Matthew in the future. There was no formal Trust. Guy Adams persisted and I became angry. I had come down hundreds of miles in order to discuss the appeal with him; not to be grilled like a criminal. I told him he was acting as if working for the Government. He thought about this and said that in a way he did work for the Government. I felt like walking out. Mr Wilkins attempted to console me, saying that Guy Adams just had to make sure the money was not from a formal trust fund, because if it was they would have to repay all the money I had given them. Oh so this was what they were concerned about!

Mr Wilkins asked me if I would go and tell Bryn to bring Matthew back in. Then I had to wait in the waiting room whilst Matthew was questioned, presumably because they didn't believe me. In hindsight I think I should have left there and then, but I gave them the benefit of the doubt. Bryn came to get me and when I returned to the room, Guy Adams said he was fairly satisfied that the savings had been ordinary savings. The discussion of the appeal started but my heart was not in it; my word had been doubted because of a headline grabbing newspaper reporter, and I resented the attitude of Guy Adams towards me.

The meeting must have lasted some three hours but an hour had been lost on the savings issue. Guy Adams' heart did not seem to be in the case any longer I felt, and perhaps he was looking for a way out. He told me that I needed a QC for the appeal. Why on earth were we here then? Mr Wilkins suggested tea or coffee, which seemed a good way of bringing this horrible investigation to an end. I went out to the waiting room with Bryn and Matthew came too. Bryn sorted out the tea and coffee machines. Whilst he was doing this I asked him what his views were on the prospects of the case. He didn't feel very optimistic, but at the same time he said he knew why I had decided to take it further. He could see that there were so many disparities in DEFRA's evidence, but he also knew they were a formidable opponent, and that I stood little chance of having a good outcome to the case. We returned with the tea and coffee.

Guy laid the large map, that had been provided for the hearing, out on the table and for the first time I was able to look at where the infected premises were marked. I realised that the first infected premise, 1779, Modrydd, the Powell's farm, was missing off the map. There should have been five infected premises shown, but there were only four. That seemed odd. Guy Adams took this on board but he seemed quite impatient with me over my view that virus could not have been spread from the valley in May 2001 up to the Beacons. I had gone through Mr Scudamore's witness statement again and again during the previous month and there were so many inconsistencies that the whole chronology made little sense. Guy Adams mentioned the 140 rams, the factor which seemed to have caused him to lose complete faith in the case back in August.

To me the 140 rams bit made the least sense of all. It turned out that it made little sense to Guy Adams or Mr Wilkins either. Mr Wilkins wondered if there had been some typographical error and that it should read as '1 of 40 rams'; not '140 rams.' Guy Adams found the whole concept laughable in a sceptical way and wondered why so many rams had been all together. This is what made no sense, and it was only later in October that I found out why.

Bryn had written up his notes of the hearing and judgment. He had also brought the details of the test results for heft 8. Guy Adams said that it was now necessary to send to Professor Brown as much information as possible to enable him to put together his expert opinion for the appeal.

The meeting ground to an end and Guy Adams tried to be positive and friendly; he seemed to realise that he had caused me unnecessary distress over our savings. We said goodbye to him and Mr Wilkins asked if we would like a lift to the hotel. I thanked him but said that we were going to get something to eat before going to the hotel. We parted company in the little street outside the Chambers and went in opposite directions. It was getting on for 5.30 and closing time for the shops, but we found a cafe for a snack before going to catch the bus out towards Clifton and the Downs.

It was a long walk from the bus stop to the hotel. On the way I kept going over and over the test results and what Dr Andrew King, of Pirbright laboratory, had written to Rosie and Alan Beat, the smallholders in Devon. Dr King has the same post as Professor Brown held at the Institute of

Animal Health and had been corresponding with the Beats for several weeks. One highly interesting piece of his correspondence related to the Brecon Beacons. He had written that they had 'received a tip off' about disease being present in a group of sheep. It seemed such a strange thing for a scientist to write and I still wonder who gave them the tip off. I had spoken with him on the phone shortly before the hearing in August and his opinion was that the countryside was a 'blood bath.' He was all for vaccination, but DEFRA was not taking heed of the experts' opinions at Pirbright either.

Anyway, we reached the hotel in the darkness and were glad to climb onto the beds and watch TV. The Blue Planet was on that evening and after watching that we sank into bed. I had phoned Glyn to tell him about the meeting and that I was not at all happy about the attitude towards me over the savings. I told him we'd ring the next day. I tried to sleep that night but lay awake for most of it worrying about the meeting.

We were both too tired to carry on to Portsmouth the next day. We had a walk round to see the SS Great Britain and the 'Matthew', but there was lots of building work and we could not get near the ships, so we looked at them from a distance. Poor Matthew became increasingly angry with me for hauling him around for no good reason and our bags were becoming very heavy. In the afternoon we caught the train home. Enough was enough for the time being.

38

Mrs Powell and Her Rams

It was not until 12 October that I plucked up the courage to phone the Baden-Powells of Modrydd. I had been talking with Mr Gatehouse that morning and I had mentioned these 140 rams. Mr Gatehouse had found it quite hilarious. He told me that they would never have had 140 rams, let alone all together. The Baden-Powells had had about 3,000 ewes on the Beacons and he went through the number of rams that would be needed for the ewes; no more than 50 to 60. 140 rams were out of the question. He told me that I should phone Mrs Baden-Powell to check it out with her.

After lunch I rang their number. A quiet elderly lady's voice answered. I introduced myself to Mrs Powell, and told her the reason for my call. She said she had heard about what I had been trying to do and sounded very supportive. I explained that I was trying to make sense of the evidence submitted by DEFRA in August, and I mentioned the 140 rams. Her tone changed. 140 rams? Yes, I told her; it was in the chief vet's witness statement. She went quiet for a few moments and then said that they had not had many rams; certainly never 140 of them. The picture was beginning to clear. I then mentioned the date of 12 July and that the rams had been at Cwm Llwch, an area of land leading up towards the Brecon Beacons. 12 July? But they had no sheep left on Cwm Llwch by that time, she told me. No sheep at all? No sheep at all, let alone 140 rams. She asked me to wait while she went to fetch her son.

Mr Powell came to the phone. He sounded very friendly and open. He was astonished by what I told him of Scudamore's statement. He confirmed what his mother had told me; they had no sheep remaining on the lower ground at Cwm Llwch after 24 June.

'Well, they've sewn us up like a bunch of kippers,' he said cynically. He asked if he could give this piece of information to the other graziers and I said that of course he could. I asked him if he'd mind writing out the information and faxing it through to me. He was quite enthusiastic and agreed to do so. I faxed him the relevant pages from Scudamore's witness statement and his very important hand-written letter came through later that day. The truth had come to light at last. Why had I been so slow to realise those 140 rams had never existed; they were a complete fabrication in order to give strength to DEFRA's argument.

Mr Powell also told me about the first group of sheep to be tested from the common land of the Beacons. He told me they had been tested on 27 June, and all results had been negative. The sheep had all been killed. The next group of sheep to be tested were the group of 159 penned on 28 June for 14 days. These were the sheep in which the one antibody sheep had been found. Neither Mr Scudamore's statement nor DEFRA's chronology had mentioned the test results for these sheep. DEFRA's chronology had simply stated, '240 sheep on the Brecon Beacons sampled.' No test results were given, and no wonder. Their argument would have fallen apart.

Mr Evans' sheep from the lower slopes had been included in these groups of sheep. Such a large number of Mr Evans's sheep up on the higher slopes near Pen y Fan had tested positive for antibodies that it seemed very odd for no antibodies to have been found in his sheep on the lower ground. All of his sheep had gone to the mountain at the same time in May 2001, so it would have seemed more than likely for there to be a fair number of sheep with antibodies on the lower slopes also. What had happened to the sheep on the higher slopes near Pen y Fan? I thought of Carwyn Jones' 'single source' and Tony Edwards' 'original point' of infection. Someone knew the answer I felt.

I faxed Mr Powell's note through to Mr Wilkins. Surely the fact about the non-existence of the 140 rams full of virus must cause Guy Adams to sit up, and believe in the case. At the meeting in Bristol he had said that the Brecon Beacons case was not the 'right case'. I still cannot fathom out what he meant by this. The only thing missing was my legal standing; everything else was there to prove illegality beyond doubt as far as I could see. Mr Wilkins was quietly amazed by the information from Mr Powell, I think, and he said that he would of course let Guy Adams know.

Guy Adams remained unconvinced even with this information and I began to lose hope that he would take the case forward with any confidence. He had told me that I needed a QC so I set out to find one.

39

Message on a Train

I told Mr Wilkins that I was not very happy with the attitude of Guy Adams and that I intended to search for a QC. Mr Wilkins said that he had complete faith in Guy Adams, but it seemed to me that Guy had had enough of the case. Why else would he have suggested the need for a QC?

In the press there had recently been mention of a QC who had a farm in south-west England. A farming magazine was joining in a case for a public inquiry and this QC was representing them on a 'no win, no fee' basis. Well, I thought, I'll try him, as he sounds a genuine soul, with an interest as a farmer, as well as being a QC.

I tracked him down eventually and spoke with him whilst he was taking a train from London to Bristol. He said that he would be glad to take a look at the case, but that he would need to communicate with my solicitor, as barristers do not communicate directly with a client. I gave him the contact for Mr Wilkins and rang Mr Wilkins to let him know. Mr Wilkins was not convinced of the need to have a QC and I do wish that I had listened to him, but I was going along the path suggested by Guy Adams, and at the time thought it the right path. The QC spoke with Mr Wilkins on the phone and said that he would go through the files and have a conference for a knock down fee of £1,000. There was some £4,000 left in the fund of donations by this time and I tried to weigh up the best way forward. There was a 50:50 chance that he would take the case on a 'no-win, no fee' basis and if he did accept the case then there was a high chance of him obtaining a judicial review for me. So I decided to take the risk. I knew Mr Wilkins disagreed, but he was agreeable to that way forward and said that he would get the papers off to the QC and arrange a day for a conference.

A date was fixed for 6 November and the venue was to be Guy Adams' Chambers in Bristol. Guy Adams had apparently said to Mr Wilkins that he would be glad to be present at the conference with the QC and that he was happy to follow his lead. I began to regret having lost faith in Guy Adams, but it was too late now to change course. The papers were already with the QC and £1,000 well on the way to being used up.

6 November soon arrived and Matthew and I were once again on our way to Bristol. A letter from a woman called Elizabeth Walls had arrived in the post just before we left for the station. Elizabeth lives near Mouswald in Dumfries and I had read about the traumatic experience that had been inflicted on her family by the authorities. Her daughter Kirstin McBride had a pet goat called Misty. On 5 April 2001, Kirstin had returned home from her work to find that Misty had been killed. Their home was in a 3km zone, and it had been decreed that Misty, a perfectly healthy animal, had to die. Whilst Elizabeth had been desperately trying to persuade the various officials not to kill the goat, a Ministry vet and official had forced their way into Misty's shed to kill her. Kirstin had arrived home to discover Misty in a plastic bag in the driveway. Poor Kirstin had then been dragged through the courts, accused of causing a breach of the peace, but she won through eventually. Another person to suffer dreadfully as a result of the 3km cull policy was Carolyn Hoffe, from Glasserton in Dumfries and Galloway. She had barricaded herself in her home, together with her five pet Dutch Zwarbles sheep. SERAD vets, together with police and armed soldiers, forced their way into her house and killed them. No official has ever been made accountable for this barbarity.

Matthew and I settled down for the journey to Bristol. I felt very nervous but optimistic too. The QC would surely not have agreed to look at the case if he did not feel there to be a good chance of success. Would he? Mr Wilkins had given him a brief outline of the case, prior to sending him the paperwork, and I would have expected him to make it clear if he felt it unlikely that he would accept it. He knew the amount left in the fund and that this was going to be used up on the conference, with Mr Wilkins and Bryn attending, and also Guy Adams.

We arrived in Bristol around noon. After buying some sandwiches from Boots we sat by the fountains in the city centre and waited for 1 o'clock to arrive, the time for the conference. As we walked up the narrow street and round the corner past the beacons, we saw Bryn and Mr Wilkins walking from the other end of the street. We waved. Off up the stairs and into St John's Chambers again and then to sit and wait by the tea and coffee machines. Mr Wilkins had brought a copy of The Western Mail with him and told me that there was an article in the farming section about the proposals for amendments to the Animal Health Act 1981. I had heard about it also. DEFRA was trying to change the legislation to make the contiguous cull policy lawful; what better proof that their actions had been unlawful?

The QC had arrived earlier apparently. Guy Adams took us across the corridor and into the room where he was waiting. He stood up as we went in and shook hands with us all. His face was rosy and he was shorter then I had imagined. We all sat down round the large table and the QC handed round a summary he had made of the merits or otherwise of my case. He asked me various questions, including what I hoped for the case and why I wanted to continue. I told him of the lie in Mr Scudamore's witness statement and how without this there was no strength to DEFRA's argument. He said that the case file was a brilliant piece of detective work and I explained how difficult it had been to obtain information from the graziers. The graziers had all fallen silent by this time. None of them had responded to a letter that I had sent, asking them for any information, such as test results and precise location of the lost flocks. The QC said that they probably looked on me as some sort of a spy. A spy? What a strange thing to say.

A woman came in with plates of sandwiches. Oh I wish I'd known that lunch would be laid on. Everyone, apart from Matthew and myself tucked into the many sandwiches and then coffee and tea arrived. We had cups of tea. I wondered what the QC was going to conclude on my case, and whether or not he was going to accept it. I had a nagging doubt. All the sandwiches vanished and talk resumed.

'I wonder if you would tell me exactly where the Brecon Beacons are,' asked the QC. This question was worrying. Here was a QC who had been paid for studying my case, and who had not checked the location of the Brecon Beacons. I almost voiced my astonishment, and said they were in Powys.

'Where exactly is Powys?' he then asked.

He didn't even know the location of the largest county in Wales? Then I realised that he was not going to take my case on; he hadn't the slightest intention of doing so. If he had the smallest interest in the case he would certainly have been doing some research to make sure he had the basic details to hand. He had been sent the A2 DEFRA map of the Brecon Beacons, which clearly showed the location of the area and so I wondered if he had made much attempt to read through the file at all. It was all so disappointing.

The QC went through the points he had noted in his summary, and one of the points was that he considered the case to be now academic. What more could I achieve? The culling had stopped. Mr Wilkins had told me that he felt that I had in fact achieved my aim in stopping the mass culls and Guy Adams echoed this now. He told the QC about the cancelled meeting at the Brecon barracks on 16 August and how he believed this was due to Carwyn Jones becoming aware that the judge had ordered a hearing that day. I tried to emphasise that even if the case had achieved the outcome of stopping the culls I wanted to try to obtain a judicial review in order to prevent the same thing happening in the future. Also, there was the issue of the costs, which had been assessed by Judge Burnton on his return from holiday. He had assessed them at £13,000 for DEFRA and £3,800 for the Welsh Assembly.

I told the QC that I was unable to meet this demand for costs as I had almost used up all of our savings and the fund of donations, and that I needed to appeal against the granting of costs. He looked at me hard and went on to say that he felt I had some very embarrassing evidence against DEFRA and in his opinion I should do a deal with them to get the costs reduced radically. I did not want to do a deal with DEFRA; not likely. I told him so.

He smiled and told me that he would not take the case. I felt like hitting him hard but instead responded in such a way that caused him to say that he was amazed at the gracious way I was accepting his refusal. If only he knew how hard I wanted to shake him and tell him how he had wasted the last of the funds. Mr Wilkins had said little during the meeting, except to agree with certain comments made by Guy Adams, and to mention the report in The Western Mail. He now looked up over his spectacles and he looked a bit disheartened too. I would not have blamed him if he had later said 'I told you so,' but of course a solicitor would never say such a thing to a client.

Mr Wilkins wanted to know where the case could proceed from there, and again the QC said that his view was that I should do a deal with DEFRA. The very thought turned me cold. Mr Wilkins said that he would telephone Jon Townsley in the next few days about this but he never did. He knew I would never do any deals with DEFRA.

So now I was to be left on my own to deal with the Court of Appeal, unless Legal Services Commission granted funding for the case. Guy Adams had agreed to carry on with the case *if* the QC agreed to take it on. He had refused so now I had to face the Court of Appeal on my own. I was capable, the QC said, of making a very good argument, but this did not make me feel any better. Flattery is worthless, particularly when accompanied by such a dismissive refusal as this.

The meeting ended. Matthew and I left the room quickly after a brief shake of hands. We waited in the corridor. Mr Wilkins and Bryn came out shortly and I told them of my huge disappointment. Mr Wilkins tried to be positive but it was hopeless. He said that he would be in contact during the next few days and we went down the stairs and back out under the archway and into the narrow street. The QC had another meeting nearby and waltzed off to that, smiling.

We didn't meet Guy Adams again. His fee for the conference was to have been £400, but he waived it altogether. He would have known that I had so little funds left and I appreciated his gesture very much.

Matthew and I boarded a train home and settled down in our seats. There was some delay in it leaving for some reason, and a man across the aisle was speaking on his mobile in an exasperated voice. He was telling the person at the other end how fed up he was with the way he was being treated by the rail company that he worked for. He was saying that there was no way he was going to give in to it. Then he quoted a few lines of the famous words of Churchill:

'We shall fight them on the beaches, we shall never surrender!'

Right, that decided it for me. There would be no deals with DEFRA. The battle would continue.

Whilst I had been trying to persuade the QC to take my case on, Elliot Morley, Parliamentary Under-Secretary of State for DEFRA, had on the same day, been persuading the Environment, Food and Rural Affairs Select

Committee that the contiguous cull had been 'essential'. He had cited the mass cull on the Brecon Beacons as 'the kind of practical experiment and practical evidence that the contiguous cull was there for,' and that 'all the evidence is that the contiguous cull works and I have seen no evidence that is has not.' The truth was a very different matter.

40

Meeting at Merthyr Tydfil

Legal Services Commission refused funding, as expected, but I put in an appeal and requested a hearing before the Funding Review Committee. The committee consists of a panel of three-six solicitors/barristers, who are in private practice and who do not work as such for the LSC. Therefore, their opinions and conclusions are seen as entirely independent of the LSC and their opinion is usually the final word on the granting of funding.

We had been given a date of 15 November and the hearing was to be held in Merthyr Tydfil at the offices of a solicitor. The hearing was timed for 2.15pm and we set off mid-morning. Glyn had changed his car in September and because of some problem with my own, we were using the 'new' one. It started to make very suspicious sounds after only twelve or so miles. Matthew wanted us to turn back and said that he could smell petrol. I could too. Glyn wanted to persevere, as he was concerned that we would be late otherwise. When we reached the tiny village of Llanbadarn Fynydd there was obviously something very wrong with the car and so we stopped and I went to find a phone to call the AA. The lady in the shop was the vicar's wife apparently and she was extremely helpful. It wasn't long before a man came out from a local garage. He had a look under the car and told us that the petrol tank was leaking and that it was dangerous. He phoned the AA and told them that we needed a car because we had to get to Merthyr Tydfil. The man looked at me and said I looked familiar. Glyn wondered if he'd seen the reports on the TV about the case, but the man felt that he'd met me somewhere. He said that a relative ran a guest-house not far from Churchstoke, near to Offa's Dyke. Her business had been affected badly by foot and mouth restrictions, he told us. He said that someone passing through their garage had told him of stockpiles of timber, back in the autumn, and he was of the belief that it had all been planned.

By 1o'clock we were in the replacement car and on our way again, but with so little time to spare. Merthyr Tydfil lies to the south of the Brecon Beacons and as we drove down through the valleys, the peaks looked down on us through the mist. I looked for sheep and felt joyous when we spotted a few groups scattered here and there, but there were none on the upper slopes. We reached Merthyr Tydfil in good time for the hearing and found the offices.

The waiting room was very drab and the administration staff worked from behind a high desk, which acted like a wall between them and the public. A woman came to ask who we were and asked me if my solicitor was with me. No, he wasn't I told her. Mr Wilkins had made no offer to be there or to send Bryn, presumably because he knew I had no further funds for them. A grey-haired man with piercingly cold blue eyes came down the stairs and asked us to follow him. He took us up the creaking staircase and on into a room where three men sat, one of them in front of a large ornate mirror. This room was smarter than the waiting room, but there was a definite air of decay about the whole place.

The man who had met us downstairs introduced himself. He was from the Legal Services Commission. He said that he was there in the capacity of someone taking notes. The man sitting in front of the mirror introduced himself as Mr Victor Ellis and the other two members of the panel gave us their names. Professor Brown's expert statement had arrived a few days previously and I asked if Dolmans had forwarded it to the panel. They did not have a copy so I handed it to them, and one of the solicitors went off to photocopy it. They all read through Professor Brown's opinion, which boiled down to an incisive criticism of DEFRA's actions. Each of them had written down a question for me to answer, and nervously feeling as if I was back at school or at some strange job interview, I answered as best I could. Then Mr Ellis, who was the Chairman of the panel, asked me to briefly explain why I wished to take the case to the Court of Appeal.

I thought of the sheep and went through my argument. Afterwards, Mr Ellis said that he could see that I felt very strongly about the whole issue. He looked at me and I could hear the ' but, I'm afraid.' I could have fallen off my chair when he then said that it was the view of the panel that, from the evidence they had seen, I 'should be granted a judicial review.' I looked at Glyn and Matthew. Had I heard correctly? Both of them were looking very pleased, so I must have heard those wonderful words.

One of the other solicitors asked me if I had applied to the Legal Services Commission's London office. No, Mr Wilkins had just applied to the Cardiff office, I told him. The solicitor told me that my case was a public interest case, which meant that I now needed to make an application to the 'Public Interest Assessment Panel' for a different type of funding. Mr Ellis asked if I had any questions to ask them and, as is the way, I could think of none. I thanked them and the interview ended. The man from Legal Services took us back towards the stairs, said goodbye and then returned to the interview room. He had made me feel very uneasy. Glyn and Matthew felt the same. His smile had been overshadowed by those eyes, so terribly cold and unfeeling.

On the way home I kept asking Matthew and Glyn if I had indeed heard correctly. I wanted to pinch myself. So far all that I had encountered had seemed to be closed doors or doors which slammed shut in my face, but now at last a door seemed to be opening. None of us could quite believe it. However, we had all heard the opinion. I wish that Mr Wilkins or Bryn had been there, because they would not have had to take my word for it later on.

41

Deception

I rang Dolmans the next day, Friday 16 November and spoke with Bryn. He was pleased that the review panel had been so optimistic and said that he would speak with the man from Legal Services about sending an application for the panel in London to consider. A few hours later Bryn rang back. He had spoken with the man from Legal Services, who had told him that the review panel had said no such thing in Merthyr Tydfil; I had made a mistake. He informed Bryn that they certainly had not told me that I should be granted a judicial review. I was furious and said to Bryn that the man was lying about what had been said in the hearing before the panel. If I had been there on my own I might have ended up doubting my own hearing ability, but Glyn and Matthew had heard it too.

I telephoned Legal Services and spoke with the man. He sounded extraordinarily unpleasant.

'Miss Hughes, you must have misheard. No one had said that you should be granted a judicial review. The committee considered that your case had little chance of success.'

What? I made it plain that I considered him to be a liar and reminded him that the panel had advised me to apply to the Public Interest Advisory Panel. Oh, the Funding Review Panel's opinion is not necessarily taken into account, I was then told. This man was deliberately falsifying what had gone on, and I could only conclude that he had been told by DEFRA to make sure I was not able to obtain public funding. I told him what I thought of him and slammed the phone down. It was disgusting how DEFRA was steering everyone in the public sector to follow their commands.

I rang Bryn again and asked him if he could make sure an application went to London, in spite of the comments made by the man from Legal

Services. He said that he would speak with Mr Wilkins when he returned to the office on Monday and get something sorted out.

Somehow I had to try and speak with Mr Victor Ellis direct. He was, after all, the Chairman of the Funding Review Committee and the person who had told me I should be granted a judicial review. Unfortunately, I had to speak with the man from Legal Services again in order to find out Mr Ellis' contact details. He was smug. There was little point, he sneered, in my speaking with Mr Ellis because the decision to refuse funding had already been made. This man was really something else. I reminded him of the fact that I had been advised to apply to the panel in London and that the review panel had been very positive about my case. He didn't know what I was talking about; I had to stifle my anger. Surprisingly, he gave me the telephone number for Mr Ellis, who turned out to be a solicitor at the firm in Merthyr Tydfil where I had been interviewed. The phone call ended. Thankfully, I never had to speak with him again.

I rang the firm of solicitors and asked if I could be put through to Mr Ellis. He was in a meeting, I was told, and the woman asked for details of my query. I explained that he had been on the review panel that I had attended and I needed to speak with him because the person from the LSC had misrepresented what had been said at the meeting. The woman said that Mr Ellis would not be able to speak direct with myself on the matter. I asked her in earnest if she would just ask Mr Ellis if he would speak with me on this occasion, as the matter was of great importance. She left the phone again, and a few minutes later came back with the same result. If I wanted though, I could write to him, she said. Okay, I would write to him then.

I did write to Mr Ellis on 8 December, but no reply was ever forthcoming. I asked Mr Wilkins if he would contact Mr Ellis on my behalf, but Mr Wilkins would not do so, as he felt it inappropriate. He had not been at the meeting and was not in a position to form an opinion or force Mr Ellis to make comment. Oh, I felt angry with Mr Wilkins. He should have been at the meeting, or should have felt able to allow Bryn to be there. It had become clear to me that a client needed their solicitor with them, as a witness if nothing else. As things stood, the person making the only record of the meeting had been the man from Legal Services and his record bore no resemblance to what had been said. The LSC guidance leaflet on hearings before the Funding Review Committee states that the member of staff from LSC 'will sit in on the hearing to act as' the committee's 'secretary.' Their representative's secretarial skills left a whole lot to be desired.

Mr Wilkins sent a letter off to the London office of the LSC on 22 November, requesting that my application be placed before the Public Interest Advisory Panel. A reply came back in early December from Mr Colin Stutt, the Legal Policy Development Manager. He informed Mr Wilkins that he had decided not to place my application before the Panel, apparently because the 'decision of the Panel could have no impact on the outcome of the application.' This seemed confirmation that there was no way that DEFRA was going to allow me to have a shred of public funding to use against them. I had been naive to hope, but I had hoped. Well, now I realised that I was well and truly on my own. Funds had all run out and Mr Wilkins now made it plain that he needed to tidily close the files on my case.

During the preceding weeks I had gathered more evidence and an application needed to be made to the Court of Appeal to request permission for this evidence to be admitted. Bryn sorted this out and also made a formal copy of the skeleton argument that I had written out on the word processor. After this, the final formality was for me to sign a form stating that I was now a litigant in person. Christmas was approaching and I sent Christmas cards to Mr Wilkins and Bryn. Mr Wilkins sent 'the compliments of the season' to us, in one of his final letters to me, and that was the end of my time with Dolmans. I was left with ambivalent feelings. Such a vast amount of money had been swallowed up, over £20,000, and Dolmans now very efficiently had closed the door, leaving me to the mercy of the legal system.

42

Christmas Preparations

On Saturday 20 December a letter came from the Civil Appeals Office at the Royal Courts of Justice. Glyn brought it upstairs with my morning cup of tea. Matthew sat on my bed, waiting to see what it said. I was almost too nervous to open it. The date of 30 January 2002 jumped out at me, as it was written in bold type. Oh they had granted a hearing! I couldn't quite believe it, as I had fully expected a refusal, after DEFRA had written to the Appeals Office, 'inviting' the Court to refuse a hearing. Glyn and Matthew were chuffed. I read through the letter. It stated that the hearing would be no more than 20 minutes and that the hearing would be without notice to any other party. That sounded very good, because it meant that DEFRA and the Welsh Assembly were not being asked to attend.

Well, this letter went a long way in making our Christmas a happy one. 30 January 2002 was in the distance for now and I tried not to dwell too much on the hearing for the twelve days of Christmas. Matthew was keen for me to practise my legal argument though, and so amongst the shiny Christmas garlands of our living room I argued my case before Matthew, who was pretending to be the judge, until he considered it to be good enough. Christmas came and went, and the end of January loomed ahead.

I booked a room in a guesthouse in Llandaff, a few miles from the centre of Cardiff. The lady sounded nice and friendly. Pat was going to stay at the same place with us, and this time I had made sure to book in good time. Dafydd Morris had said that he would come to the hearing too, and planned to set off at 5.30 am to catch the early train from Caernarvon.

Again and again I went through the file of extra evidence that had gone to the court in support of my case. In late October/early November I had become obsessed with the maps of DEFRA and the Welsh Assembly. Both of them had shown just four infected premises and the first IP had been omitted. The A2 DEFRA map showed an area numbered as 5b, east of heft area 5, but this area was not numbered at all on the Welsh Assembly map. Heft 5b, according to Mr Scudamore's witness statement, was one of the hefts where many sheep belonging to Mr Evans had been found to have antibodies at the end of July and it had been given an infected premises number of 1907. Why then, was heft 5b not even numbered on the map of the Welsh Assembly?

Our computer did not have the software required to convert the A2 image from the Welsh Assembly web site, into a reduced j.peg copy and Mr Wilkins had been unable to obtain one from the Welsh Assembly. All I had was a quarter of the map, which was not of much use. DEFRA had complained to Dolmans that I was still writing to officials, but a certain Colonel in Cardiff had been very helpful when I had phoned him about the map. He had apparently been in charge of distributing it on 3 September 2001. The Colonel was very affable and said that he would post me a copy.

I had also managed to find a friendly official in the Animal Health Office at Llanishen, near Cardiff. He had posted me an A4 coloured copy of a large-scale map, which clearly showed the infected premises in the valley and this map correctly showed five of them. The map was produced by GI Services of the National Assembly for Wales Agricultural Division. If this map was able to show the correct number of so-called infected premises, then why was infected premises number 1779, the initial one of the Libanus outbreak, omitted from both the DEFRA map and the Welsh Assembly map published on 3 September on the Assembly web site? A possible answer did not come to light until several months later.

The map from the Colonel had not arrived by 29 January and so I had to make do with the quarter of the map off the computer. Matthew was coming with me as always bless him, and we arrived in Cardiff late evening. BBC Radio Wales had telephoned me before I had left to ask if I would go along to give an interview on 'Good Morning Wales', on the morning of the hearing. The BBC Wales studio is in Llandaff, so even though the interview was scheduled for a time far too early for me, I agreed. I was not expecting to sleep a wink the night before the hearing, and so an early interview was not a problem.

My dream of not having barristers from DEFRA and the Assembly at the hearing had crumbled. Mrs Mason-Buggs, of Case Management Group C at the Civil Appeals Office, had kept DEFRA informed, as directed by a Master Venn, and it seemed that they were intending to have a barrister present. After making enquiries I found out that DEFRA had written to the Court requesting that they be kept informed and so the 'without notice' hearing had been neatly hijacked. Mrs Mason-Buggs was not the most helpful of souls, but she did forward me a copy of the letter that she had sent to DEFRA on 21 January 2001. In the letter she noted DEFRA's concern as to whether the matter had been listed with or without notice, and she informed them that Master Venn had stated that, 'the respondents may attend by counsel if they wished; however they would do so on the basis that the court has not 'REQUIRED' their attendance and they are at risk as to their own costs and should not assume that a costs order will be in their favour.'

So, I just had to patiently wait and see if barristers turned up; I fully expected them to be there.

The Welsh Assembly had posted me a brief skeleton argument that they had submitted to the court. In one section of the argument they cited my claim that they had been taking decisions in relation to the culling. Their argument ended by stating that,

'even a contrary finding would not necessarily make any difference to the conclusion that there are no arguable grounds for a judicial review but in view of the conclusion to which the learned judge was inevitable driven by the evidence this issue does not arise.'

Well, Mr Justice Stanley Burnton had certainly seemed driven back in August 2001, but unfortunately more by the opponent's false evidence than anything else. It was like a thorn in the memory.

The Assembly and DEFRA had been served with all the documents containing the extra evidence that I wished to rely upon for the appeal hearing. One piece of evidence had been a record of minutes of an Assembly Chamber Session on 8 May 2001, that I had come across purely by chance, whilst rummaging through the Assembly website.

In this record there was a very enlightening conversation between Rhodri Morgan, the First Minister, and Elin Jones, an Assembly Member. Elin Jones had asked Mr Morgan if he believed that a full investigation was needed into the foot and mouth disease as soon as it cleared and whether he believed the investigation should consider the confusion between MAFF's powers and those of the Assembly. Rhodri Morgan's reply practically jumped off the page at me. He told Elin Jones that it was, 'not confusion but flexibility. It is clear that dealing with animal welfare was not devolved to the Assembly. We are clear on the law; it was not part of the settlement. Despite that, as a matter of flexibility and in light of our relationship with central Government, it was prepared for us to deal with the matter in Wales. **De facto, the matter was devolved.** Therefore, does Elin believe that we should have nothing to do with the matter because it was not legally devolved? No one would take the Assembly seriously if we said that we in Wales should not deal with this matter because it was not included in the legal settlement and was therefore a matter for MAFF only. No one would accept that.'

Well, here was the First Minister clearly stating on record that the Assembly had 'de facto' dealt with the matter of foot and mouth disease in Wales. He had not mentioned any agency agreement, and I had not seen any written evidence to support this claim. This statement of his was an admission that the Welsh Assembly had indeed been dealing with the matter and not MAFF/DEFRA. How I wished that I had discovered these minutes back in the summer. Even if I had though, I doubt if Mr Justice Stanley Burnton would have taken much notice, if any at all.

43

Bird Song

We arrived in Cardiff early evening on 29 January 2002, and found the stop for a bus to Llandaff. The guesthouse is in an area of Llandaff called Fairwater. I asked the bus driver if he could let us know when we arrived there, as I didn't know the area. We ended up getting off at the wrong end of Fairwater Road and had a long walk to the part where the guesthouse lies. As usual we had loads of bags. We had had to bring clothes and shoes suitable for a courtroom and the bags grew heavy as we walked up and down Fairwater Road, trying to find the guesthouse. The numbering system of that road is chaotic, with no apparent pattern or continuity, but eventually we stood outside the gate of the pretty Victorian terrace. The hallway was lit up and we walked up the short pathway through the garden and rang the bell. We could hear footsteps coming down the stairs. A figure walked down the hallway and opened the door. It was Pat! She had arrived there a couple of hours earlier, she told us, and Win, the owner, had had to go out before we arrived. Pat took us upstairs and showed us our room. Then she said that she had brought a bottle of wine with her, and would I like some too. Oh absolutely Pat! So we had a drink and Matthew had a little rest whilst I showed Pat the quarter coloured Assembly map. 'Yes, they said the Beacons were red with blood,' Pat said as she looked at the bright red of the hefts that had been culled.

The summer of 2001 seemed a long time ago, but at the same time it was all so vivid. The hearing back in August seemed as yesterday and still does two years later. Pat very strongly believed that the Brecon Beacons case had stopped the culling on the Beacons in its tracks. Well, something had happened for sure, as there had been no further outbreaks or culling in Wales since August. Pat told me that we had ' beaten the bastards Janet!'

and that I should feel proud for taking the case on. I did feel proud but I also felt that something of a greater power than I had worked through me and helped from the beginning. As soon as I had committed myself to the case, it was as if this great positive force had taken over and worked through everything. Call it Christian belief, or a faith in the power of God, but I shall never forget the strongest feeling that someone was at my side and at the side of those animals, working away to stop the dreadful evil.

We went off down Fairwater Road in the moonlight to search for a place to eat in Llandaff. Llandaff is a very pleasant place with a quite famous cathedral. There were not many places to eat that were open, I suppose due to the time of year, but we found a pub and had a snack, and then walked down the long road back to the guesthouse. The thing that remains in my mind was the bright moon lighting our way and Pat telling us that her little cat Kiwi had jumped out of the bedroom window. She was fine but sounded a crazy little thing. In the moonlight we walked back up the stone path of the guest-house and went to get ready for bed. Soon after we got back there was the sound of the front door and Win, the owner, had returned. She is a lovely lady and made us feel very at home. She is slightly deaf though and the volume of her TV made me glad when she retired to bed!

She asked us what time we would like breakfast, and looked most curious when I mentioned that I was being collected at 6.30 am to go to the BBC Wales studio. She looked slightly perturbed when I mentioned that I had to be in court by 10 am and I decided not to elaborate that night. After Win had turned off her TV we tried to settle for sleep. Our room window, which was at the back of the house, looked down over the city and the Millennium Stadium was lit up like a ship out at sea. The hours went by. Matthew sounded as if he was asleep and I tried so hard to get to sleep, but spent the entire night, as expected, tossing over and over, unable to find a peaceful place in my mind away from the fears of the next day. In August I had had a barrister, but tomorrow I was to be relying on myself and that gave me no rest. I was quite glad when 6 o'clock came and I had to get ready for the taxi. Matthew wanted to come along of course and woke up fast. It was still dark when we went down and out of the little front garden. The birds had started to wake up and a few quiet notes came from the trees lining the road.

The taxi driver was very nice and whisked us quickly to the studio, which is quite close to the guesthouse. Soon we were sitting waiting for my turn to go into the studio. Matthew was fascinated; he watched the people in the sound-recording room deftly managing all the buttons and switches, making sure that each person went on air at the correct time. I was so nervous that my mouth kept going dry and I had to ask for a glass of water. My turn came all too quickly. The girl in the studio was very laid back and they all made me feel at ease. She asked very pertinent questions about antibodies and asked me how I expected the hearing to go later that morning. I hoped the right answers came out.

By the time we returned to the guesthouse dawn was almost approaching and the birdsong had increased. The blackbirds were singing joyously in the light rainfall and other, smaller birds had joined in. We thanked the taxi driver then went in to have a rest on our beds, and wait for breakfast time. Win was very interested in what was happening. BBC Wales, and court? She wanted to know what was going on. We ran through what had been happening and in between cooking scrambled egg and making toast she listened avidly, asking questions now and again. A lady who came to help her with cleaning, arrived and Win proudly told her that I had been on the radio and that I was fighting the Government. Oh dear, was I that mad?

After breakfast we prepared to leave and I went to pay. Win didn't charge for Matthew and said that it was her way of helping 'the cause.' It was people like this who made the whole thing feel worthwhile.

There was a knock at the door. The taxi had arrived. We bundled in and Win waved us off.

44

Fire Drill

The friendly taxi-driver was interested in our legal activities. He said he was totally on our side and he thought the present government dreadful. We arrived at the Civil Justice Centre and the driver said, ' I wonder who the cameras are waiting for? Oh I think they're waiting for you.' We got out and he wished us luck. The cameras clicked away much to my absolute astonishment. The reporters asked me a few questions and it was then that I saw a lady standing against the wall of the entrance, holding a sign painted in red lettering, stating; HELP SUPPORT JANET. She looked wet and tired. I went to say hello and she said she was Sue, from Essex. She had phoned me a few days before to say she'd be coming with a few others to give me support. We went in.

We went to check in at the entrance desk and then along the corridors to look on the notice boards for the courtroom number. Yes, here it was, Lord Justice Latham was hearing my case in court number 7. Sue had started to dry out and we had a bit of a chat. She told me that she had been staying in a motel just outside Cardiff, and had been waiting outside the court in the rain since about 8.30 am. I immediately felt that here was a true friend, and I didn't feel quite so nervous any longer. Oh God, I then saw two figures approaching, in their legal gowns, one of whom was familiar. They came over and introduced themselves as Mr Keith Bush, counsel for the Assembly and Mr Gwynne Griffiths, a solicitor from the Welsh Assembly. Mr Gwynne Griffiths, I now realised, had been the rosy-faced man who had sat looking embarrassed and unhappy during the hearing back in August 2001. They went off into the courtroom to prepare. Lucky them!

A stout woman wearing a black hat and black winter coat with a red flower in it came over and gave Matthew and I a hug. It was Marlene

Morgan from Abergavenny, who is a farmer's widow, and incensed by Carwyn Jones. She had supported me since summer 2001 and had phoned to say that she would come to the hearing. Then Dafydd Morris arrived just in time. He had managed to catch the early train, he said.

The court usher came to call people into court. She looked at Matthew and said that children were not normally allowed to be present. I told her that Matthew had been with me in the High Court in London and there had been no problem, and so she went to ask another court official, and returned to say that Matthew could come in as long as Justice Latham agreed. We filed into the courtroom and I went to sit at the front bench, along with the legal pair from the Assembly, and a barrister who I recognised from the hearing in London, who was there for DEFRA. The three of them, all wigged, had taken all the places with the book rests, even though they weren't even 'required' to be present. Oh well, I thought, try and intimidate me then! The DEFRA counsel came up to me with a sly grin on his face. He told me that I needed to start by asking Lord Justice Latham for permission to adduce my further evidence. 'Thank you,' I replied, thinking at the same time that I would decide what I would ask the judge, not this slippery DEFRA barrister.

The court usher called out for everyone to stand. Lord Justice Latham appeared and went to take his place up on the bench. He wore thin rimmed spectacles and had greyish white hair beneath his wig. He looked a kindly soul. The room fell silent, apart from some shuffling of papers by the barristers. My mouth was becoming dry and I shook as I poured the water from the glass decanter on the bench. Mr Justice Latham was addressing the courtroom, and then said, 'Miss Hughes, it's your application.' A voice somehow far away from me, answered, 'Yes.'

Lord Justice Latham looked down on me and smiled slightly as he said, 'I've read the papers and therefore I am familiar with the facts of the case, and it's your application then, for me to grant you permission to apply for judicial review. Is there any other evidence that you wish to place before me today?'

'My Lord, the evidence I've put forward a few weeks ago, then there's a map- it was not forthcoming from the Assembly so I had to take it off my computer; it's from the National Assembly web site. There is also a letter from the Brecon Beacons, which arrived yesterday.'

Lord Latham laughed and told me that I couldn't have received a letter from the Brecon Beacons.'

I think it was at this point that my nerves were forgotten. 'No, it's from the Brecon Beacons National Park Authority regarding the hefts on the Beacons.' This letter had contained the words 'culling pens', a possible slip of the writer. The pens had been for testing so they all had said, but here was their true description. The reason I wished to include the letter was that it contained confirmation that DEFRA had numbered the hefts. 'Would I be permitted...?'

Lord Justice Latham asked me if the barristers had seen the document, and I told him that the map was on a public information web site.

The DEFRA barrister intervened. 'We haven't had sight of it. If Miss Hughes is wishing to rely on it, then we would strongly object to...'

'I do not need to rely on it.' I cut in. I was not going to be bullied by this barrister, who had behaved shockingly back in the High Court in August.

Lord Justice Latham asked me what I wanted to say. 'Is it Miss Hughes, or Mrs Hughes?'

'Miss. Since August, the time of the court hearing in London, I have been studying evidence from DEFRA which I was not able to peruse until 10 minutes before the hearing. I have found several important discrepancies in relation to the evidence of the Chief Veterinary Officer. I want to appeal because I don't feel that Mr Justice Burnton had the correct information put before him.'

'I understand; inaccuracies.' answered Lord Latham. 'No, LIES', I wanted to shout out.

Then I pointed out that my sheep had been on heft 17, a heft in danger of being culled, from what Mr Vajda had said to Judge Burnton. I told him of the sheep that had been tested and culled on 14 August some 5 km west of the Beacons. He listened and made notes.

'Let's move on,' he then said. 'What's the position now? What are you seeking to obtain from the court?'

'I'm trying to obtain some sort of judicial review, a declaration, to look at how DEFRA or the Assembly implemented their policy.'

'I'm not sure it's very easy for the court to do that; deal with the questions you bring. The only thing that the court can do is look at the lawfulness of it. It can't debate the functions of the decisions...'

'I realise that the court can only look at the law and that there are a great many facts to this case, but the law that applies to this case is the 1981

Act.' I was not going to allow Lord Latham to bring an end to proceedings this quickly.

Mr Bush, counsel for the Assembly, was sat next to me and I could tell that he was scribbling away furiously. Pat, who was sitting with us, told me after the hearing that the barristers had been looking very worried at some stages and that there had been no smirks on their faces throughout. I was surprised when she said this and pleased too.

There then followed a discussion about animals with antibodies as opposed to live virus, and the slaughter powers held within the Animal Health Act 1981. Lord Latham wanted to know what was wrong with the Secretary of State determining the distance for slaughter and his remarks caused quiet uproar. Marlene started muttering loudly behind us, and Lord Latham said, 'I don't want any talk except from Miss Hughes.' I wanted to turn around to say a few positive words to Marlene, but I had to continue battling on with my argument.

I cited the evidence from Professor Brown. His statement confirmed that the test results had shown no spread of disease. The judge asked if there was anything else that I wished to say, and I told him that I could go on for days. I could have. There was so much that the public needed to know, and that had failed to come out in the press. My submission ended by telling Lord Latham that it was necessary not just to draw a blank over what had happened on the Beacons, but to look at the situation under the 1981 Act.

'You've made your point very clearly Miss Hughes. The question is are these proceedings the place to raise the issues you wish to raise?'

'This is the only place to raise the legal issue.'

'Is this a legal or scientific issue?'

'In this case,' (somehow he had to understand), 'the science is inextricable with the law. The law is precise; science is precise.'

Lord Latham wondered if enough was known about the science and antibodies and I cited the information in the Northumberland Report of 1968, about animals with antibodies not being killed by the Ministry. Then he said that the Ministry hadn't said that antibodies were infectious, 'if you follow me,' he finished. Well, maybe not, but why then were they killing millions of animals with antibodies? I told him that the tests carried out had been for antibodies, and mentioned the fact that the IAH at Pirbright was able to test for virus within 4 hours. At last I had been able to get this out in a court of law.

Lord Latham had looked serious and troubled throughout my submission. The atmosphere of the room was very tense. I realised that I had sat down the whole time; I had felt so tired from lack of sleep that I had forgotten to stand up. Oh dear, I hoped he didn't mind. He hadn't seemed to mind. He began his summing up and his judgment. He went over the powers held within the 1981 Act, and described the wording of schedule 3 which relates to slaughter powers, as 'very wide.' Oh dear, here we go again, I thought, he's going to refuse. His judgment lasted some 20 minutes, and in it he noted the 'significant factual discrepancies' in Scudamore's statement. He stated that 'the only evidence that there was any exposure to foot and mouth disease was the finding of antibodies on certain of the sheep which were contiguous to the hefts where the culling took place.' He went on to say:

'Indeed, it may be that, on a detailed and thorough investigation of the evidence in the present case, it will be found that it would have been more appropriate for a decision to have been taken to pen the animals in respect of whom there was any concern and to test, using the tests which Miss Hughes has identified both in the evidence before me and in her submissions, on the basis that that would provide a securer basis for determining whether or not the animals in question had indeed been exposed to disease by being able to identify the existence or otherwise of active infection.'

At this point in his argument, Lord Latham began to stutter and you could see that his hands were shaking, because the leaves of the papers he was holding were shaking. His words stopped flowing and he could hardly come out with some of the words. He started taking about the ambit of the Minister's powers and how I could only invoke the powers of the court by way of judicial review if it could be shown that the Minister had acted outside the scope of those powers. I should take my complaint to the inquiries at present 'in train,' he said. The inquiries to which he referred were inquiries, which were to become an absolute whitewash of events of 2001. Lord Latham carried on stuttering to the very end of his judgment, when he said that, 'It seems to me that there is no arguable case that the decisions were unlawful, which is the question that I have to answer. I would accordingly refuse this application for permission.' There was the silent bombshell yet again.

There were sighs and groans from the people in the room, and then the fire alarm went off and we were all shepherded out of the courtroom. Several folk later said they believed this to be a deliberate ploy to prevent uproar at the judge's decision. We shall never know that for sure, but I do have my own suspicions.

45

Endings and Beginnings

We were summoned back into the courtroom after a few moments and Lord Latham returned to his place. He had given his judgment, and had recovered his composure. He now asked if any of the barristers wished to say anything. None of them did. He asked me if I had anything else to say. I said that Yes, I did. I told him that the hearing was supposed to have been a 'without notice' hearing and that none of the barristers should have been there. Lord Latham seemed to think I was referring to costs, which I wasn't, because he said, 'Miss Hughes, you don't have to worry about costs. There is no order for costs.' I'd forgotten about potential costs for this hearing. But what of the £16,800 apparently awarded against me last August? That issue had not been dealt with at all, but I was too weary to even think of asking the judge about this. He said how nice it was to come out of London and that was the end of the hearing. We all stood up and Lord Latham left the room.

I sat down and glanced around the room for the first time. All the barristers were smiling, but their smiles seemed to be smiles of relief and not mocking smiles like back in August. Mr Bush, the Assembly barrister, looked extremely relieved and he very politely said goodbye to me. Oh I felt gloomy and failure had hit me again. I turned to Matthew and Pat. They were very disappointed. I started to gather the papers together and back into my bag. There was another hearing coming up and we had to vacate the courtroom, so I hastily grabbed everything, including our travel bag under my seat, and went back out into the corridor.

A reporter came to ask if I would have a few words with her. She was from the Press Association and asked similar questions as had been asked back in the summer. I told her that I intended taking my case to the

European Court of Human Rights, as I felt that justice had not been done. The reporter thanked me for the interview and left. Dafydd Morris came to sit down next to me. Matthew was having a chat with Marlene and several folk were engaged in discussion about the hearing. Dafydd told me firmly that I must not attempt to take the case any further; I had done all I could, he said, and I had not been given justice. We talked for a long while and court officials walked past, looking slightly annoyed that we were still there.

Time came to leave; it was getting on for lunch-time and someone suggested a place to eat around the corner. All I wanted to do was get on a train and go home, but I was hungry too and didn't want to appear rude. Marlene came up and gave me a hug and said how disgusted she was with the judge. She left to catch her train. Then, we all piled out of the court, and walked around the corner to the eating place. It turned out to be a fairly noisy bar, which did not allow children, but they agreed to waive the rules if I made sure to 'keep him out of sight.' Goodness knows how I was supposed to do that, but we went to sit around a table and Matthew sat between us, trying not to be conspicuous.

Pat did not know what to make of it all. The result of the hearing had been as expected really but it was still a bitter blow. Meals were ordered and tiredness crept up on me, as I sat there with the music sounding louder and louder. We finished our jacket potatoes and salad, and I wondered how long it would be until I could extricate Matthew and myself from this place without being rude. Sue must have seen how tired I was because she said she'd have to leave soon and said she was taking us back home. I told her we had a return train ticket but she insisted on driving hundreds of miles out of her way. She would not take 'No' for an answer. So Sue went off to get her vehicle and said she'd meet us up the road. Astrid, a lady who had come from Cumbria to show support and Pat came with us.

Astrid wanted to take photos of us and so we walked back near to the court and had some photos taken with the masts of the Millennium Stadium in the background. Sue brought her land rover to meet us and after hugging Pat and Astrid goodbye, we took off for home. It felt as if I had known Sue for years, even though we'd just met. She didn't know Cardiff and I was very unsure of the correct road out of the city but we managed it, and soon the city was left behind.

It was not long until we were passing Merthyr Tydfil and then onto the A470, the road through the Brecon Beacons, the place of so much heartache.

We stopped off at a place called Garwnant Visitor Centre, run by the Forestry Commission, as we all needed the loo. The place seemed deserted and we went to see if anyone was there. There was a strange atmosphere to the place; amongst the smell of pine trees, there was a feeling of desolation and dreadful sadness. We found a door open to the main building, which is a study centre for school visits, and went in search of someone. There were voices coming from one of the rooms and we knocked on the door. A woman came to see who was there, and seemed very surprised to see visitors. Some sort of meeting was in progress and a few people were sat round a table. The woman said that the centre was closed for the winter but we were welcome to use the facilities. As we walked back out through the educational study room we gazed at the large mural along one of the walls. The painting was of the nearby valley of Gwaun-nant Ddu and the scene showed the various species of wildlife that might be seen there.

I was glad to leave that place even though it was beautiful. Sue and Matthew had felt uneasy there too. Darkness started to fall as we left the National Park and drove on up through Powys. We arrived home about 6pm and I wanted Sue to stay the night. No, she would get back. It was such a very long way though. No, just a cup of tea with us and then she'd be on her way.

Glyn was glad to see us but very fed up at the ending with the court. I had phoned him from the noisy bar. He told me that a large envelope had arrived that morning and went to get it. Inside was the map from the Colonel. It **would** arrive the very day of the hearing. I briefly explained to Sue about the maps and about how there seemed to be irregularities in them; such irregularities that made me suspect the maps to have been drawn up prior to the 'outbreak' at Libanus on 23 June back in 2001. This map, I noticed, was different from the map on the Welsh Assembly web site. There was still no 5b mentioned, but the map showed more numbered areas; up to 55. Area number 53 was marked with red and this showed that sheep had been culled from there. The area was the forest area of Garwnant. No wonder we had felt so ill at ease in that place. The beauty of the place had become overshadowed by the recent murder of the sheep.

Sue set off on her long drive to Essex. I felt sad to see her go. She has a very large animal sanctuary and I felt very grateful to her for having taken the time to come over to support the case.

We had some supper later on and I had a more thorough look at the Colonel's map. Unlike the Assembly map and the DEFRA map, this map did show all five infected premises in the valley. It also differed from the Assembly map in that several hefts showed different status of testing, even though the maps had apparently been published the same day, 3 September 2001. On the Welsh Assembly map hefts 20, 18, and 17 were awaiting testing, but on the Colonel's map these hefts had already been tested and found clear. If the maps had in fact been published the same day the test results would most surely have been identical. Using a magnifying glass it was possible to make out the name of GI Services, SVS, (State Veterinary Service), Llanishen. Again, like the map sent to me back in November, also drawn up by GI Services, this map showed the correct number of infected premises, but there was still no heft numbered as 5b. Oh, these maps were doing my head in and I was too tired to consider them any further that night.

We all went to bed with very mixed feelings. The legal case may have ended as far as the British courts were concerned, but there were other ways to tackle the evil. We had made some wonderful new friends along the way and I now had to set about applying to the European Court of Human Rights, (ECHR). I had to accept this ending as a beginning of something else.

46

Resource Planning Team

In February, Mr Townsley of DEFRA Legal Department, wrote to ask how I intended paying their costs. I wrote back, informing him that I was taking the whole matter to the ECHR. He then wrote to say that this fact did not mean that I did not have to pay their £13,000 costs. I then informed him that the matter of the costs was also being placed before the ECHR, and that I did not see why I should pay any sum to DEFRA in view of their huge waste of tax payers' money over foot and mouth disease. I heard nothing more and put DEFRA's demands to the back of my mind.

I planned to get started on my submission to the ECHR by late spring. I had six months in which to complete it and so I tried to have a little bit of normal life in between finding out a bit more. These maps bothered me. I knew there was something adrift with them.

The map accompanying Mr Scudamore's witness statement appeared to be a prototype for the later maps of the hefts on the Beacons. No infected premises or hefts were marked. Heft number 16, I couldn't help noticing, had the '1' leaning slightly sideways and it looked as if someone had applied the numbers by hand with Letraset, or something similar. Again, there was no area numbered as 5b.

In early February I enlisted the help of a very friendly cartographer who lives in Shropshire. He was glad to do some research on the maps. He told me that he and his wife had visited the area of Ystradfellte, the area of waterfalls to the west of the Brecon Beacons, back in late May 2001, and how he had noticed the great number of sheep grazing in the area. This period of time would have been soon after sheep had been allowed back to the area from wintering in Pembrokeshire.

I faxed the various maps through to him and he rang back a while later. Two of the maps were road maps, he told me, which he felt was an odd type of map to use. Surely they would have referred to a larger scale type of map, instead of a road map, for pinpointing areas of land where sheep grazed? The map put in by DEFRA on the day of the hearing had been from a larger scale Ordnance Survey map, and the areas of the land were clearly designated. Why two different types of maps? The cartographer took on board the strange method that had been used to draw up the 'heft' areas and he agreed that the method used looked 'somewhat old fashioned.' Therefore, my suspicions grew.

During that week I also contacted a cartographer from Powys, and faxed the 'prototype' map through to him. He rang back and said that he considered the map to be ' a horrid map.' He told me that the method used was crude and in his opinion no government department would have used such a method, not recently anyway. The map started to annoy me more and more. How was I to get to the bottom of it? I rang various offices of DEFRA, in search of a cartographic unit. An official in a London office of DEFRA told me that everyone who had worked on mapping for foot and mouth had now left; they had been temporary. I mentioned the reference of OLK 8170, which was the file code, and immediately met with a wall of suspicion and secrecy. Oh, that would be an internal reference and why did I need to know? I told the woman that I was trying to obtain a colour version of the black and white copy, and that so far there had been no knowledge of this map in any DEFRA department. She said that she was unable to help. I bet she was.

The nearest I got to the origins of the map came from comments made by an officer in Powys County Council mapping department. I faxed him the map and he told me that he remembered it coming through to him as an e-mail attachment. He had been away at the time, he said, but he thought that it had been sent around the end of June 2001, just after the first outbreak at Libanus. He said that he recalled how there had been plans to test sheep on the whole area of the Beacons immediately after the first outbreak at Libanus, and the map, as far as he could recall, had been sent by the State Veterinary Service in Cardiff or Llanishen. So the hefts then, which had been numbered by DEFRA, had been marked out and numbered by the end of June 2001, at the latest.

The map of the hefts, published by the Welsh Assembly, was also based on an OS road map. The map had a key, which was titled 'Brecon Beacons.' The key related to the hefts, coloured in red, blue and green. Red related to 'cleared of animals', blue to 'awaiting blood testing', filled-in green to blood testing results negative, and unfilled green to 'blood tested awaiting results'. This was one of the maps where the first infected premise had been left off. (Map of the Hefts). The map had been drawn up by the Resource Planning Team, CAPM NAWAD, (Common Agricultural Policy Management, National Assembly for Wales Agriculture Department.) So I went in search of the relevant cartographic unit. I rang through to the main switchboard of the Assembly in Cardiff and asked for the Resource Planning Team's number. The person had no knowledge of that department; there certainly was no department of that name in the Cardiff offices of the Assembly, I was informed. They put me through to the cartographic unit at Cardiff and a man there wondered if the unit was the one at Aberystwyth. I was given a number and phoned.

A woman answered the phone and I asked for the Resource Planning Team. She sounded slightly vague; Resource Planning Team? 'Oh, you mean for IACS?' No, I told her, I was trying to obtain a copy of a map of the hefts on the Brecon Beacons published by the Resource Planning Team. (IACS stands for Integrated Administrative Control System, and farmers have to complete forms for payments in relation to land that they own.) Hefts on the Brecon Beacons? She went off somewhere to ask someone about the map and returned saying that no one knew about this particular map, but that someone in another section might be able to help. So, she put me through to a man in the GI Services department. Ah, this was the department that had drawn up the map sent to me last November by the helpful officer at the Animal Health Office and the map from the colonel. I explained to the man in GI Services that I was trying to obtain a full copy of the map published by the Welsh Assembly, which showed the hefts on the Brecon Beacons. He told me that he thought he knew the chap who had gone down to the Beacons to draw up this map, but that he was not sure and would get back to me.

Later that afternoon he rang back. Yes, he had spoken with the man concerned and this was the map in question. He was not sure though how to obtain a full copy, as the map was no longer on their system. I asked him about the hefts and who had actually drawn up the areas.

'You know, the numbered areas don't stand for actual land owned by anyone,' he said, 'The areas were numbered so that they knew where to go to shoot the sheep.'

Now the road maps made sense; they must have used road maps so that the slaughter men and the truck drivers knew where to go. It was all so sickening.

Temporary numbering systems were also applied throughout the country to many premises and land grazed by susceptible livestock. Understandably, it was necessary to know the exact location of animals for disease control purposes. There were several series of numbering systems. Sometimes, two or three temporary holding numbers were applied to the same premise or area of land, as shown by the map references. This seemed slightly questionable to me but again, could be explained by there having possibly been different numbering systems used by regional Animal Health Offices and by DEFRA in London.

However, one particular series of temporary numbers stood out. When I checked the map reference for number 4522, I found that it applied to the lane outside Modrydd farm, where animals had been culled on 23 June 2001. This seemed very odd to me because the earlier number of 4517 in the same series had been applied to a map reference for a tree-lined lay-by near the Storey Arms, alongside the A470. This lay-by was adjacent to the land where the many thousands of healthy sheep had been slaughtered in the specially constructed pens in late July and early August 2001. It was from this lay-by that the dead sheep had been trucked to rendering plants in England. How could this location have been given an earlier number than Modrydd farm?

Documents also show that plans were afoot for the siting of the pens on the Beacons, prior to the initial outbreak at Modrydd. Changes appear to have been made for the location of the pens, but the final location had been determined by 23 June 2001.

I discovered that heft 5b had in fact been the southern area of heft 5, (Map of the Hefts). The map reference for the infected premises of 1907, (heft 5b), was SN999197, and this matched the location of the triangle for the IP on heft 5. The central area of the Beacons had only been numbered as heft 5b on the map supplied by DEFRA for the hearing. The area was not numbered on any other map, including two other State Veterinary

Service maps and I can only conclude that it was numbered in this way to give strength to the argument for culling heft 21, where Mr John Phillips' large flock had grazed. The geography of the area shows that there is a natural barrier between heft 5 and heft 21. There is the very high ridge of Craig Gwaun Taf, the most easterly area of heft 5, where Mr Evans' flock grazed and there would have been negligible risk of any contact between the flocks from hefts 5 and 21. In any case, prior to the sheep on heft 21 being culled the authorities knew perfectly well that there was no infection in the sheep on heft 5; merely historic antibodies.

It later transpired that test results for the sheep on heft 5b had in fact returned as negative; not 61 positives out of 811 sheep, as stated in Mr Scudamore's witness statement. These figures were actually the second test results for heft 5. An epithelium sample taken on 28 July from a sheep, (ear tag no.0 1087) on heft 5b had returned negative results, but in spite of this knowledge the heft was declared an infected premises, IP 1907. 1328 sheep from heft 5b were slaughtered on 31 July and blood samples taken when the sheep were killed returned negative results on 6 August.

We drove down to the Brecon Beacons in early March 2002. The spring sun lit up Pen y Fan and Corn Ddu, the twin summits, but the whole area felt so sad, as if in mourning. I wanted to find Llwynbedw, the area at the base of Cwm Llwch, where so many sheep had once grazed in peace before the building of the pens. In the fading afternoon we drove up one lane after another, until it seemed that we would never find the correct lane up to Llwynbedw. There was a turning from one lane that seemed to match the OS map route to Llwynbedw and this lane took us up to a gate, beyond which was a rutted track. To the right of this track there was a large pen with MAFF posters along its side. Little streams ran down through this small wooded valley, and we could see small groups of sheep up on the lower slopes amongst the trees. It was beautiful, but the overwhelming feeling was of a great loss.

There was the outline of a farm across a field, and I wondered if it was the home of the Phillips. The map showed a car park at Llwynbedw, but there was no car park here. There was just this large pen, with sheep droppings around it and inside it. The colour of the ground looked wrong in places; areas of it were tinged with patches of dark reddish brown. It was some eight months since the sheep had been coaxed into the culling pens, so this pen surely could not be that type of pen. But the Ministry Foot and Mouth Keep Out posters were attached to it. Had someone forgotten to dissemble the wicked object?

The slopes of the Beacons were turning to a dark grey in the dimming sunlight, and we decided to leave this sad place, with the streams and the small bunches of sheep. Glyn drove through the gate to turn round and as I was shutting the gate after him I looked back up the track through the trees and a little white Jack Russell terrier was running down towards us. She came over to me, wagging her tail, and seemed to want to come away with us. I told her to go home, and ran off to the car. Carefully we started off, and in the rear window we could see the little dog frantically trying to keep up with us. She ran after the car all the way down the long lane, and then gave up. I wondered where she had come from. Was she the little dog belonging to the Phillips? My imagination does tend to run away with itself sometimes, but it was as if the little dog had not wanted us to leave.

The following week we wrote to the office at the National Park, asking if a pen was still at Llwynbedw and the reply came back to say that there were still three pens in the Beacons, and that one of them was at Llwynbedw. So we had found the right place after all that day; perhaps this was what the little dog had been trying to tell us. We should not have left, but instead should have followed the little terrier up through the trees and on up to Cwm Llwch. I wonder if we would have found anything else up there, except a terrible sadness.

In May 2002, I had one last attempt at obtaining a copy of the Welsh Assembly map. I rang the Aberystwyth number again. A different lady answered the phone. Resource Planning Team? Oh, that was now called GI Services. It felt as if a piece of the jigsaw had finally been found. I asked how long the resource planning team had been known as GI Services. The lady told me that the Resource Planning Team had been changed to GI Services at the end of March 2001. So this was why I had received such vague responses to my enquiry; there was no longer any such department as the resource planning team. The lady advised me to write with my request for a copy of the map and on 27 May, Andrew Bradick of GI Services rang. He told me that my letter had been placed on his desk and that he could not understand why because he had been out of the country for most of 2001, and therefore knew nothing of the map in question. I explained that it had been published on the web site of the Welsh Assembly and that I was unable to print off a complete copy of it from my computer, and he told me that he would print a copy off and send it to me. I also asked him about the date when the department changed its name and asked if he could send me this in writing. He sounded baffled by my request, but a fax came through a few minutes later, verifying that the 'Resource Planning Team became the GI Services Branch, CAP Management Division, Agriculture and Rural Affairs Department, National Assembly for Wales on 1 April 2001.'

The first outbreak to affect the Brecon Beacons had been the outbreak at Libanus on 23 June 2001. How then, having changed its departmental name at the end of March 2001, had the Resource Planning Team managed to draw up a map of foot and mouth on the Brecon Beacons? In response to my general inquiry on dates of Assembly maps, Mr Bradick considered it an 'outside chance' that maps, drawn up later than 1 April 2001 would bear the name of Resource Planning Team.

'They would generally bear the name of GI Services,' he had told me. The jigsaw piece fitted, and the picture was becoming increasingly dark.

47

The Last Resort

In between trying to find out more about the maps, I had begun the submission to the ECHR. I had downloaded the application forms off the ECHR web site, and the procedure seemed fairly straightforward. The good thing was that there was no cost for making the application, and better still, that even if the court rejected the application there would still be no costs. So, there was nothing to lose. I had no lawyer or barrister and so set about writing the statement of facts. An application has to be made under certain Articles of Violation, and the only Article which seemed to apply to my situation, seemed to be Article 6, Right to a Fair Hearing. The hearing back in August 2001 had certainly not been fair or just, with my being unable to read the opponents' evidence prior to the hearing, and especially as that evidence had contained false information. You have to be a 'victim' of a violation under each Article, and I did feel like a victim after that hearing; a victim of the system. There were other possible Articles that applied but only as a potential victim.

It took a few months to complete the submission and I included any aspect of the case that I felt applied. Under Article 34, which is the Article that gives you the right to submit your complaint, you need to show victim status or potential victim status, and the ECHR apparently informs a claimant early on if their submission is unlikely to fall under Article 34.

I decided to write a letter of introduction, which is a method often used, and a couple of weeks later an air mail letter arrived, containing a set of application forms and a reference number for my submission. As soon as the court receives the letter the six-month 'clock' stops effectively, and you have a bit more time in which to make sure you have made your case as sound as possible.

Glyn and Matthew gave the thumbs-up for the submission, and I posted it at the end of June 2002, together with two large files containing all the documentation of the case. A week later the postman called at the gate with a large Royal Mail sack, containing the parcel to Strasbourg. The Post Office clerk had apparently used the wrong method of posting, and the parcel had been rejected. It was a good thing, I thought at the time, that I had been early in sending it to the court. So, off it was sent a second time, this time with the correct special delivery postage of nearly £40. I kept my fingers crossed that it would not arrive back at the gate. It didn't.

After checking with the court that the documents had arrived safely I set about enjoying Wimbledon. The ECHR takes at least a year to make a decision on admissibility and so it would be June 2003 before we would know the outcome.

DEFRA Legal Department remained silent on the issue of costs and for the remainder of the year we crossed our fingers and hoped for the best. Christmas came and went and January 2003 arrived. As with all folk, sad times mingled with happy times and we felt that we were beginning to return to a time of greater normality at last.

PART THREE

THE AFTERMATH

48

The Two Crows

On Monday 27 January 2003, I looked out of our kitchen window and in a tree in a neighbour's garden sat two large crows. The tree had been partly cut down, and was completed felled a few weeks later, but on that day the two crows sat, one on each of the large remaining branches. I mentioned them to Matthew, as they sat there for such a long time. They must have been there for an hour or more, and then when I looked again the tree was once more on its own.

In the early hours of Tuesday morning I woke up, sweating with fear. I could not get back to sleep and could not understand why I felt so dreadfully worried.

At 10 am some TV repairmen were due to call, and when they arrived I was embarrassingly still in my dressing gown, due to my awful night. They could not find any problem with the TV and left. The dogs were shut in our conservatory, and after the men had gone Glyn went to the local supermarket and I got on with making a late breakfast. Matthew wanted a fried egg and I poured out a bowl of corn flakes for myself. He wanted to fry the egg himself and I started to pour the milk on the corn flakes. Then Matthew said, 'Mum there are two people at the window.' So there were. I thought they might be Jehovah's Witnesses.

I left Matthew to see to his egg and went to see what they wanted. There was a woman and a man, and they were holding files. Who on earth were they, I wondered? Our front door opens into the porch, and the porch was crammed full with pot plants brought in out of the cold weather, so I opened the front window instead.

'Hello, are you Miss Hughes?' asked the woman in the raincoat.

Well, I am Miss Hughes, so I told her, 'Yes.' I wish I had pretended to be someone else.

'Miss Hughes, we are here on behalf of the Department of the Environment, Food and Rural Affairs, to collect £17,000 owing to them.'

Matthew had left his egg and come to join me at the window. I was trying to mentally digest the words the woman had just uttered. I could not understand it at all, because I had not heard a squeak from Mr Townsley at DEFRA, since March 2002, almost a year ago. The vague order that Mr Justice Stanley Burnton had made back in October 2001 had assessed DEFRA's costs at £13,000 but now I owed £17,000. How?

I explained to the woman and man, who apparently were Sheriff's Officers from Cardiff, that I had not heard from DEFRA for almost a year, and that I had placed the case with the European Court of Human Rights. This information seemed to cause them some discomfort, especially the man, but they were adamant that they were going to list my possessions to the value of £17,000. I told them that I was not going to allow them in, as I knew my rights on that, and so they told me they would list the belongings outside in our garage and our shed.

The weather had worsened and in driving rain they went off round our yard to list my car, then disappeared into the garage and the old cow shed. They were looking at Matthew's toy jeep and his quad bike. I called out of the window that they couldn't list those, as they belonged to Matthew. They called back through the pelting rain that they were listing them. Matthew began to cry. Tears rolled down his face and I told him not to worry, everything would be okay. They were not going to take any of his things.

I ran to the phone and rang Tuffins, the supermarket up the road and asked them to put out a message for Glyn, as he was needed back at home. Then I went back to the front window. The man and woman were nowhere in sight. Matthew told me they were still in the shed. They re-appeared clutching their files and returned to our window. The woman handed me the list of possessions they had listed, which included 'child's toy jeep and quad bike', and the man handed me a form to sign, called a 'Walking Possession Agreement'. I told them that I did not wish to sign anything, especially an agreement for my goods to be seized, and the man said that I didn't have to do so. So I didn't. When I told them that I intended fighting against this possession order the man told me that I had five days in which to make a claim to the court. The woman wrote down the claim number of the warrant and the number was the same as my old judicial review application. Surely, DEFRA should have a different claim number? No, this was the High Court claim number I was told. The man asked the woman, 'Jan, can we give Miss Hughes this other form?' She said she didn't see why not, and put various papers in an envelope. Then they left and we stood and watched them until they disappeared round to the main road.

Matthew had gone ashen and I had started to shake. Glyn was still not back and I was stifling feelings of panic. Matthew's fried egg had gone cold in the pan and he was too upset to eat anything. What was I to do? I had to get myself organised somehow. I thought of Rob and Frank of HTV. Should I ring them? Oh yes, Matthew thought that a very good idea. Frank answered the phone. He could hardly believe what I was telling him. Rob was away in London, he said, but he would ask Heath Jeffries, another reporter with HTV, if they could come out to do an interview. Frank rang back and said they'd come to our home soon after lunch. Frank is a lovely, reassuring man, and I began to feel less panicky after speaking with him. I also rang Karen, who back then was the local reporter on the Shropshire Star. She was flabbergasted and extremely angry and told me that she would ring up and find out anything she could for me. Karen had followed the case right from the start back in the summer of 2001 and she had written many reports on its progress. This time it was us personally who were in DEFRA's firing line, not the poor sheep.

I made a cup of tea for us and then Glyn came back. We didn't quite know how to explain to him what had happened whilst he'd been at the supermarket. He could not take it in at first. I showed him the papers that they had left. There was the unsigned walking possession agreement, inventory of possessions, and the form that the man had asked if they could give me. This form was a ledger, dated 28 January 2003, and had columns showing amounts of costs and interest and fees. At the top was the name of a solicitor, scribbled out with biro; Napthen, Houghton Craven. I later found that they were a firm up in Preston, and they knew nothing of the warrant, when I rang them. There was a warrant number of MON 41 cited in the ledger that they had left me. Shouldn't I have been given a copy of the warrant? I had been too stunned to ask to see the warrant and I had also omitted to ask for the credentials of the bailiffs. They had left no contact details. I only knew they had come from Cardiff. I could have kicked myself. Five days would be gone in a flash and then someone would be back, presumably with a large van, and would force their way into our home to clear us out. It was too frightening to consider.

Frank and Heath arrived around 2 o'clock. Frank wanted film of us with Matthew's toy jeep and quad bike. The fact that these bailiffs, or whoever they were, had seized possession of Matthew's belongings made Frank very angry. They were not allowed to do that, he thought, and Heath Jeffries agreed. Frank said they would put the piece out on the tea time news. I felt so grateful to them for coming out so quickly. I had let BBC Wales know of what was happening, but the chap on the news desk had wanted to send me a video to tape the bailiffs taking my belongings. I told him that there was no way I was going to allow that to happen.

After Frank and Heath had left I started sending e-mails to friends. Sue in Essex simply could not believe what was happening. Mavis, who runs a large animal rescue centre up near Aberdeen, said she would put out messages for help and said that I should contact Alistair. Alistair MacConnachie, up in Glasgow, runs Sovereignty, 'a Journal for National Self-Determination'. He was fired up about the bailiffs and wanted to put a piece on Sovereignty web site. Had I any photos of us that were suitable for copying? I had a black and white one of us that Bonnie had taken back in September so I scanned it and e-mailed it to him. Yes, that would be fine. Alistair is a very positive person with a great many influential contacts, so I felt a load better after I had told him about the bailiffs.

The day ended with no progress on discovering the origins of the bailiffs or the writ. By the time HTV and the photographer from the Shropshire Star had finished with the interviews that afternoon, it was too late to start ringing courts. That would have to wait until the next morning. During the evening, I looked on the internet and downloaded any piece of material that might possibly be of relevance. I found the form for Walking Possession and discovered that I should have been given a Notice of Seizure, containing information about the seizure of goods, and the contact details of the Sheriff. Fear of losing all my belongings was turning into a great well of anger. How dare these people sneak about our home without warning, trying to seize my car, which was essential to my teaching career, and how dare they try to seize Matthew's toys. On top of that, they had not even had the decency to leave the Notice of Seizure, as required by law.

49

The Elusive Writ

The next morning I telephoned the High Court to try and find out about the warrant and the bailiffs. I rang the Administrative Court Office and spoke with a helpful woman who looked on the court records to find out the date of issue of the warrant. All she could find was the record of my judicial review application. She could find no records at all for the warrant. I explained that I had not been provided with a copy of it, and that the only reference I had was MON 41.

'The bailiffs must be private bailiffs,' she said, 'because otherwise there would be a record of the warrant.'

I told her that all I knew was that they had come from Cardiff. She sounded sympathetic.

'A warrant from the High Court would bear a seal of the court,' she went on, 'and if one had been issued here, there would be a record of it.' The only thing she could suggest was for me to phone the High Court in Cardiff to find out if the warrant had been issued there.

So I phoned that office, and the woman checked the records. She could find no record of a warrant having been issued against me, and said that the High Court in London would certainly have a record if it had been issued there.

'They have to pay a fee,' she told me. 'There would be a record of the fee and the date when the writ was issued.' She suggested that I contact the Sheriff's Office for Powys, as 'High Court writs are normally dealt with by Sheriff's officers.' I had no idea where the Sheriff's Office for Powys was, and this lady did not know either. 'Try your local county court,' she said and thanking her I rang off.

After several fruitless phone calls, I managed to speak with a court official at Welshpool County Court, who was aware of the Sheriff's system. 'The Sheriff's Office is here in Welshpool,' I was informed. But those bailiffs had come from Cardiff. Anyway, he gave me the number for the Sheriff's Office in Welshpool. The number sounded familiar and turned out to be the number of our family solicitor. A woman there explained that they used to be the Sheriff's Office but that the system had been centralised and transferred to Cardiff and she gave me the name and number of the firm. At last I had the means to get hold of these bailiffs.

I rang immediately and recognised the woman's voice on the other end as the bailiff who had visited us the previous day. She sounded incredibly annoyed that I should have discovered their whereabouts. I said that I needed to have a copy of the warrant or writ and she refused. 'We are not obliged to do that,' she told me, in a cold voice. I had to try and keep calm, but anger was boiling up inside. I told her that I had been informed that I should be provided with a copy and that furthermore, the High Court in London had no record of one having been issued. She sighed, as if realising I was not going to give up, and told me that she would contact Mr Townsley at DEFRA. I mentioned the fact that they had not even provided me with any contact details the day before. 'Oh I am sorry Miss Hughes, the weather was so bad that we forgot.'

On Wednesday 29 January a solicitor telephoned to offer help. He said that someone had contacted him and had said I might need help, but he would not divulge the name of that person. 'Have you sent in an application for a stay of execution?' he asked. I had not heard of this process, and told him I hadn't known what to do. He suggested that I make an application as quickly as possible, and told me that around 10% of applications are successful. Well, anything was worth a go, so I thanked him very much and rang the High Court for a form.

BBC Midlands Today rang that afternoon, after seeing Karen's report in the Shropshire Star. They wanted to send a reporter and cameraman round the next morning. The publicity was keeping the bailiffs at bay for the moment, I felt, so I was happy for them to come round. It had snowed in the night and the air was very chilly. A reporter called Robin did the interview and Ian, the cameraman told us how he had read the newspaper report about Matthew's toy jeep and quad bike the previous evening, and had asked BBC Midlands if they would pick up on it. They were with us for more than two hours and our new kitten Lottie was made famous on camera. We had films of Matthew and I taking Bess, our sheepdog for a walk up the lane in the snow, and films of me by the window and films of us padlocking Matthew's vehicles in the garage. By this time Glyn had bought large padlocks for the gate and the sheds, to serve as a warning that if bailiffs returned they would have to force entry, in public by now. All the reporters asked me to let them know as soon as there was a sign that the bailiffs would return. Frank from HTV had given us his home number in case of emergency, so all in all we felt shielded by the media from these enemies.

The Midlands Today evening news carried our story, and there was little Lottie basking in the limelight of fame, rolling around next to Matthew, who was filmed doing his Maths.

I had sent a letter to Mr Townsley by special delivery, offering to pay £30 per month. Our income was very low, as Glyn had retired in August 2002, and we were just not in a financial position to pay more. The offer would probably be met with ridicule and rejection, but it was an offer. Somehow, we had to stall these bailiffs with their dangerous, elusive writ.

50

The Umbrella Man

The weekend passed with no more unexpected visitors. Rob from HTV
phoned on Monday morning. He told me he had been shocked by what
Frank had told him on his return from London. Was it okay to come
around to do another interview? Rob had been incredibly supportive of
me in 2001 and 2002, and this support meant a great deal. Prior to 2001,
I had not dealt very much with reporters. There had been a couple of
occasions, back in the 80's when as a student I had joined an anti-road
demonstration, as a member of the local Friends of the Earth group, and
in the early 90's, when we took towels down to Pembrokeshire to help the
oiled sea-birds. Since 2001, however, I have realised just how large a part,
reporters play in their stories of people's lives. I have absolutely no doubt
that in the absence of all the media coverage of the bailiffs' visit, we would
have been left staring at empty rooms, devoid of our belongings.

Rob and Frank came along later on Monday morning. We had a long chat
about it all. Rob said his long weekend in London had been very cold, with
loads of snow there. He could not believe what had happened to us, he said.

Karen, from the Shropshire Star, had phoned DEFRA and the Sheriffs
Office, to seek some answers for her reports, and she acted as a sort of go-
between, in a sense. The PR bloke from DEFRA was not very friendly, she
told me. In fact, he was almost hostile to her questions, she said. I could
quite believe it.

Christopher Booker had written a piece about DEFRA sending in the
bailiffs in his column in the Sunday Telegraph on 2 February and there was
a photo of Matthew on his quad bike and me on his jeep, with Holly, our
little dog bouncing about. According to a reporter on the Daily Post,
DEFRA had been very angry at this article. I could understand why, because

it helped scupper the bailiffs' return. They had been due to return on Tuesday, 4 February and then DEFRA informed reporters that they were considering my offer and were holding off the bailiffs until Friday 7 February. On 4 February Mr Townsley wrote to inform me that they were considering my offer of payment, and that they had asked the Sheriff's Office not to continue against me whilst they were considering the proposal. I had to be thankful for this. At least we had some time to play with now.

A UKIP organiser, from Herefordshire, had phoned to offer help and he arranged to visit us in the afternoon, on Friday 7 February. I felt incredibly weary that day, as if a heavy boulder was weighing me down. We were all tired. Matthew was waking up in the night talking of bailiffs. It was awful and it had to be ended, but not by giving in to DEFRA. Donations had started pouring in from all over the country and over £2,000 had been sent to us already. I was amazed at the kindness of total strangers. The situation was taking its toll on all three of us, and without that help the emotional toll may well have been too much.

The High Court had not responded to my application for a stay of execution. On the occasions when I had telephoned the court office, I had been informed that they had no knowledge of the application. What was the reference number of my claim? What was the number on the writ? When I told one court official that the only reference I had was MON 41 he had asked, 'Well, don't you have a copy of the writ?' When I had explained that I had not been given a copy of the writ, he told me that I should certainly have a copy, in a tone that seemed to blame me.

I grew worried. What had happened to my application? I wrote a letter to the court office and awaited a reply. When I checked our bank account it showed that the cheque for £25 had been processed, so where was my application?

Friday 7 February arrived. In the afternoon we got ready for the man from UKIP. The dogs started to bark in the conservatory. I looked out of the front window and was horrified to see a huge red van reversing up to our gate. Fearing the worst, I ran out of the porch door. Glyn had gone out to see who it was and I could hear him talking with the driver. Then Glyn was starting to unlock the padlocks from the gate and the van was reversing into the drive. It couldn't be bailiffs then. Matthew was watching from the window and I felt sweaty and cold at the same time. A shortish, chunky man jumped out of the van and I could see he had a file in his hand. Oh God, what was going on?

He walked with Glyn up to the porch and introduced himself as Jim, from UKIP. Thank goodness for that! As we shook hands, I told Jim that I had feared he was a bailiff, as this was the day that had been mentioned for their return. He breezed in and made himself at home. One of his previous jobs had been a bailiff, he told us, and over a cup of tea he went through the papers, sifting out the ones he wanted to look at more closely.

'You were very lucky that they left without taking your stuff with them,' he told us. 'They could have taken your things because you refused to sign the walking possession agreement.'

He also told us that I was entitled to see a copy of the writ. He wanted to know what had happened back in 2001 when the judge had made the order. Who was my solicitor back then? Mr Wilkins, of Dolmans, I said. Right, he would ring him. Mr Wilkins might well have heard about the bailiffs' visit because he buys The Western Mail and on Saturday 1 February there had been a half page article about what had happened, with a photo of me behind our padlocked gate. The gate looked like some sort of wooden fortress, due to the clever way in which Richard, the photographer had angled the picture.

Mr Wilkins was in his office, and had indeed heard about the visit from the bailiffs. From Jim's words and nods, we gathered that Mr Wilkins needed some time to recall events of the case and some time to retrieve the files from their archive. He would do that within the next few days, he told Jim. Poor Mr Wilkins must have thought that I was either too upset to phone him or offended somehow. Neither was the case; Jim was just very organised and knew exactly what he needed to do and who he wanted to speak with. He told us he would ring the Sheriff's Office on Monday and tell them that there was nothing worth having!

Before he left he talked about how he used to live in London and had a market stall, making and selling umbrellas. He was a 'Mary Poppins,' then, coming to our aid in our hour of need. He thought this very funny. I never quite understood the reason for him turning up in the huge van, but he has always been referred to ever since as the Umbrella Man.

He did phone the Sheriff's Office the next week and the High Court. I am not sure how much sense he obtained, but his intervention seemed to do the trick for the time being.

51

Discoveries

On 14 February, Mr Townsley wrote to inform me that DEFRA had considered my offer and regarded it as inadequate. Mr Townsley pointed out that it would take more than 36 years to pay, at that rate. He informed me that they were prepared to accept payment of £150 per month or if I agreed to pay £200, then they would waive all the interest charges, thus taking the debt back to £13,071,75. He wrote that their offers remained open for 14 days and if they did not hear from me 'within this time, we will consider our options.'

Well, we could not afford to pay £200 a month, almost a quarter of our monthly income, or £150 a month and I wrote to let him know this. I also asked if he would let me know what he meant by 'consider our options.' A very terse reply came back, signed by someone other than Mr Townsley. 'Consider our options,' I was informed, ' means just that.' The letter writer also informed me that DEFRA had a 'responsibility to safeguard public funds.' DEFRA had obviously chosen to forget that they had forced their way in on the case back in August 2001. I had written to request a copy of the writ and whoever had written the letter stated that a copy of the writ was enclosed. It wasn't.

We tried to relax a little over the weekend, but it was difficult. Even though DEFRA had written to say that they had called off the bailiffs for now, I found it hard to believe. The writ was always with us, a continual threat. On Sunday we had some visitors. Phoebe and Dennis had read of our troubles and came to bring us a big tin of biscuits and a donation. The gulf that had fallen between us since spring 2001 fell away, and that was one blessing that the writ brought. It was lovely to see them again. Their anger and sadness over the killing of their healthy sheep was very visible.

On 25 February, Glyn went to Welshpool to collect an item of post that had been returned to the Post Office, because it had no stamps on it. He paid the fee and brought it home. The only postage mark on it was Welshpool Post Office. On opening the envelope, I found that it contained my application forms for the stay of execution. There was no covering letter and the front page of the application had written on it, 'refused by Ungley, 6 2 03.' I had received no responses whatsoever to any of my three letters that had been faxed through to them. They really did take the biscuit, not even having the decency to post my forms back to me properly. This was supposed to be the High Court, a place of justice for all?

On 4 March, the Sheriff's Office sent a copy of the seizure notice, the form that should have been given to me on 28 January. The notice was dated 3 March 2003 and the warrant number was MON 45, instead of MON 41. How many warrants were there, I began to wonder? In the accompanying letter they referred to my further request for a copy of the warrant, and stated again that they were not obliged to supply me with a copy. I had spoken with Ms Parsons, the bailiff, a few days earlier, and whilst again refusing to send me a copy of the writ, she said that she would provide me with details of the debt.

'On 11 October 2001 it was adjudged in the Supreme Court of Judic...Judica?..'

'Judicature?' I had offered.

'Yes, that's right, Judicature; in the Supreme Court of Judicature,' she had continued, ' that the claimant Ms Janet Hughes do pay the defendant £13,000, execution costs of £71.75 and interest to be charged at 8% per annum to commence on 11 October 2001.'

I could not understand it. What Order dated 11 October 2001? Had she made a mistake? No, it stated 11 October 2001. She had obviously been reading from the writ, because of her difficulty in pronouncing the word 'judicature.' The letter accompanying the seizure notice had this same statement, referring to the Supreme Court of Judicature, and 11 October 2001. What was going on?

A special delivery packet arrived on 6 March. Inside was a letter from Mr Townsley, apologising for not sending the writ and here at last was a copy of the writ itself. It felt quite exciting in a perverse sort of way. I settled down with my morning tea and studied the Writ of fieri facias. During the course of being a litigant in person, I had felt the need to purchase several legal books, and this phrase had caught my attention some months back. 'Fieri facias,' 'you should cause to be done.' Fleeting fears had crossed my mind when I had read of this type of writ of execution, because of its extreme powers of seizure.

Hand written at the top of this writ was MON 39, not MON 41, as I would have expected. It bore a seal of the Administrative Court Office with a date of 5 November 2002. For some reason they had sat on this writ until almost the end of January, before sending it to the Sheriff's Office. Ms Parsons, the bailiff, had told me that awful Tuesday morning, they had only received the writ the day before; 27 January. There was no claim number apart from my old claim number and the claimant appeared to be me. This was not as it should be. Common sense told me that. The defendant was stated as being DEFRA and the wording of the writ was such that the Sheriff's officers were 'commanded to seize' the defendants goods and so on, in other words DEFRA's! This original wording had been crossed out and my name had been hand written over the top. The initial date had appeared to be 29 October 2002, and again this date had been crossed out and replaced by 5 November 2002. There was no wording to match what Ms Parsons had read out; no mention of Supreme Court of Judicature.

I turned the page to the 'Schedule'. At the top of the list was stated: Date of a Judgment or Order, and next to this a date of 11 October 2001 had been typed in. 11 October 2001? Here it was again. I had thought the date of the Order of Assessment had been 9 October 2001. In section 3 of the list, 9 October 2001 was typed in as being 'Assessed costs.' So, where was the order of 11 October? Why had Mr Wilkins never sent it to me? During the course of the day and the following day, I emptied all the bags full of documents that had accrued since August 2001 and searched for an Order dated 11 October 2001. I also e-mailed Mr Wilkins to ask about this Order or Judgment.

The Order that Mr Justice Stanley Burnton had made on 9 October 2001 eventually emerged from a bundle of papers on the Friday afternoon. This was titled, 'Order on the Defendants' applications for assessment of their costs', the one that DEFRA had cited as assessment of costs, in the schedule to the writ. I read through it carefully, and realised that this Order contained no order to pay. Then I went back to the file that contained the Order of 21 August 2001. This Order 'ordered' three things: 1. Permission be refused; 2. First defendant (DEFRA) to serve schedule of costs by 2pm on 22 August 2001; and 3. Written submission or oral hearing on costs by 2pm on Friday. There was no order to pay on this either.

I decided to e-mail Mr Townsley at DEFRA to ask if he would be able to send a copy of this Order dated 11 October 2001. He replied quickly, stating that he would fax a copy through to me. A few minutes later the phone rang and I went to watch the piece of paper come through. It was crazy. My heart was pounding over a piece of stupid paper. A piece of stupid paper that I already had; the Order dated 9 October 2001. So I e-mailed him back to say that he had sent me the wrong Order, but by this time it had dawned on me that it was highly unlikely that there was any other Order at all. Mr Townsley e-mailed back, confirming that there was no Order dated 11 October 2001, and that a typographical error had been made on the writ.

So, the High Court must have processed the writ without checking, as required by law, the various Orders that allowed the writ to be issued. There appeared to be no Order for me to pay DEFRA, but this needed to be checked by a legal professional. I also needed some answers from the High Court. The lady in the Administrative Court Office listened carefully to my queries, and checked the computer records.

'There is no record of an Order to pay,' she said. 'There is a record of the Order dated 21 August 2001, and then it looks as if some papers went to Mr Justice Stanley Burnton for costs assessment, but there is no record of any Order to pay. Just the Order of refusal.' She said that she would check the files in storage on Monday and get back to me.

On Monday morning I rang the High Court, anxious to know if the lady had found anything. She answered the phone and said that she was in the middle of writing to me about the matter.

'I'm afraid,' she said, 'that I have found a Judge's Order regarding costs dated 9 October with a following Order of 5 November attached to a schedule of costs from 11 October 2001.' The lady said that she was so sorry and she sounded genuinely sorry. In her letter, which she faxed through a few minutes later, she wrote that she was very sorry.

The various documents faxed their way through; the Order of 9 October 2001 and the writ from 5 November together with the schedule containing the non-existent Order. What the hell was going on? I rang the lady back and explained that there was still no Order dated 11 October

2001. All she could do, she said, was ask her superior officer, Mr Les Peters, about it. Her final words were,' I hope you are able to expose the flaws and use them to your advantage.' I hoped so too.

When I studied the copy of the writ sent by the High Court I realised it was an exact copy of the one sent by DEFRA. Scribbled at the bottom of the schedule page was 'change authorised by Les Peters.' What change? Change of dates from 29 October to 5 November? But this copy also had MON 39 at the top and the date 11 12 2002, exactly the same as DEFRA's copy. How was it possible for the High Court to have a copy of the writ after it had been to the Sheriff's Office? As soon as a writ is received by the Sheriff's Office it is endorsed with the date and 11 12 2002 must have been the date of receipt of this particular writ. I had to speak with Les Peters, to find out what he had meant by 'change authorised.' I rang. According to Mr Peters, he knew absolutely nothing about this, and said that he was angry that someone had forged his name on the writ, as he had authorised nothing. Was he giving me the facts? I shall never know.

On 24 March I telephoned the High Court again. I had received no reply from Mr Peters to my letter of 17 March, in which I asked him for some clarification of the situation, and I felt the need for a proper explanation. We had been living under the threat of bailiffs returning for almost two months and I wanted to get to the bottom of this writ. A man answered the phone. I asked if I could speak with Mr Peters.

'Oh, he's busy at the moment. Can I help?' The man's name was Stuart Jarman, a colleague of Mr Peters. I started to explain my query about the writ, and Mr Jarman knew of the situation. 'There is no record of it. In fact, a copy was sent in later.' Later? By whom? Mr Jarman would not elaborate, and went off to fetch Mr Peters. Mr Peters sounded hassled. Yes, that was correct. They had no record of any writ being issued by the Administrative Court Office. Well, how was there a copy of it in the file then? He did not know. When I rang back to ask Mr Jarman about the writ being sent in to them later, he said that he had no recollection of having said such a thing. Oh well, they had, in any case, provided the proof themselves, by sending me the copy of the writ held in their files, which showed as clear as daylight that it had in fact been sent in 'later.'

52

Pound of Flesh

Zac Goldsmith, editor of the Ecologist, had placed an appeal in one of the monthly issues of the magazine, and a great deal of support had been generated. I had first spoken with him on 21 February, when he had phoned up to offer help. He has many contacts, and one of them is a firm of solicitors in London that specialises in class actions and human rights issues. They agreed to help, and a few days before Matthew's birthday in late March, one of the partners, David, took me under his wing really. That's how it felt, even if it does sound too sentimental. He asked me to fax through the most relevant documents and off went the Orders and the writ to him.

One of the first things David noticed was that the writ bore the wrong seal of the court. He told me the writ should have been issued in the Central Office of the High Court, as it states on the front page, but that this seal was of the Crown Office, or as it was now known, the Administrative Court Office. This seemed fairly fishy to him, and very fishy to me. Anwen, a reporter on our local County Times had visited us back in February to do a report on the bailiffs, and I had sent her a copy of the writ. She always felt that it was not genuine. Indeed, it was now emerging, that this writ had been sealed in the wrong office by someone who did not appear to know the correct procedure. No wonder the High Court had no record of having issued the damn thing and no wonder it had taken so long to obtain a copy of it.

David went on to discuss the Orders. He agreed that neither of them was in fact an 'Order to Pay' and therefore DEFRA had no grounds for obtaining this writ. Even though I had suspected this for several weeks, I could not quite believe it. This must have been why DEFRA had cited the non-existent Order dated 11 October; they also knew that there was no formal Order against me. This writ could have resulted in my losing every treasured possession I owned. The thing that made me most angry however, was the apparent collusion of the High Court in all this. What if the writ or warrant was for officials to enter premises to kill animals? Would the High Court collude then, and grant a warrant in the absence of the necessary legal grounds? A warrant for seizure of possessions is bad enough, but a warrant for seizure of animals is much, much worse.

The High Court finally started replying to correspondence, after David spoke with several court officials over the phone at the end of March. As expected, they would not admit to any procedural irregularities in the issuing of the writ. The 'slip rule' became their easy excuse. The slip rule allows for genuine clerical errors to be amended, but there is a danger for the rule to be misinterpreted. In a letter from the Court Manager of the Administrative Court Office I was asked if I wished for the original Order of 21 August 2001 to be amended to make express reference to costs. Well, I would have thought that only a person of unsound mind would wish for an Order to be changed into an Order for costs, especially when they live on a financial borderline, as we do. So I refused to request that.

March passed into April. By early April I had found a local firm of solicitors to act on my behalf. Eirwen, a friend near Swansea, who had been of great support since the start of the case, had persuaded me to have another go at Legal Aid and so I did. Citizen's Advice Bureau in Ammanford, South Wales, gave me some telephone numbers, and said that a firm in Newtown specialised in public law. So I had phoned Flanagan and Jones, and had spoken with a Mr Adrian Foulkes, a legal executive with the firm. The prospect of taking on DEFRA had not seemed to cause him any problems, and an appointment was booked.

Glyn, Matthew and I had gone along with all the documents of the case, and the more recent events, and we found that we were allowed 10 hours of solicitor's work free of charge. It was only when I had handed over the problems to Adrian that I realised how tired I had become. Waiting for a move from DEFRA Legal Department had been like a sword hanging over us; we had been at the mercy of their whims. Now at least we had some form of protection in the form of Flanagan and Jones.

Help flowed from all sides. A barrister, who had sent a donation of £500, gave his legal opinion free of charge. Documents were faxed or e-mailed over to him, and even at Easter weekend he sent e-mails with suggestions for a way forward. He was of the opinion that there was an implied Order for costs, if not a formally drawn up Order. However, he also believed that the writ had been improperly issued, and that I should make a formal complaint to the High Court. He felt that DEFRA could be forced to accept a greatly reduced amount.

On 22 May, Adrian wrote to the Sheriff's Office to request a copy of writ MON 45. He mentioned the fact that there appeared to be three warrants: MON 39, the number on the copy sent by DEFRA and the High Court, which had never appeared on any letter from the Sheriff's Office; MON 41 and MON 45. An amazing reply came from the Sheriff's Office, on 11 June, stating that warrants 'MON 39 and MON 41 are null and void.' The only warrant in their possession was apparently MON 45. Adrian wrote to ask for a copy of this writ and at first the Sheriff's Office refused. After being informed that they had a legal duty to provide this information, they sent a copy of what was supposed to be writ MON 45. You could see where MON 39 had been erased. Every minute detail was identical to writ MON 39. Writ MON 45, with its reference to the 'Supreme Court of Judicature,' was never forthcoming, perhaps because it would have shown more than mere typographical errors. So it did seem that the bailiffs had visited us in January on the legal basis of a null-and-void writ, MON 39. Mighty confusing and disconcerting.

Adrian applied for public funding. He had sent numerous letters to DEFRA and the Sheriff's Office but the replies that had come back were full of the same nonsense as had been sent to me. The Sheriff's Office had agreed to remove Matthew's vehicles from their list some weeks earlier, but they refused to remove my car. It remained on their seizure list until the end.

On 10 June I decided to ring the European Court of Human Rights to check if any decision had been made. 'Yes,' said the lady in her French accent, 'A decision was made by the court on 5 June. Your application has been refused, I am afraid.' Oh, what a huge disappointment it was, even though I had known the chances of acceptance were slim. Matthew was very philosophical about it. 'Mum, he said, 'if they had accepted it we might have had this hanging over us for another four years, and they might still have rejected it after all that.' He was quite right.

The letter from the court arrived on 19 June. It stated that, amongst other things, my application did not comply with Articles 34 and 35. These are the Articles, which allow submissions to be made. So, even though DEFRA had placed false information before the court in August 2001 and bailiffs had been sent to seize all my possessions, under an improperly issued writ, the European Court of Human Rights had found no violation and furthermore, that I had not been a victim.

The tennis season had started and I became immersed in it, determined to try and put the case to the back of my mind. All doors seemed to have closed and the writ was still there like a black cloud over us all the time. Five weeks had passed since the application for funding had gone to Legal Services Commission and still no decision had been made. I had rung the Chester office now and again, and then towards the end of June I was told that the case had gone to the lawyer there, and that a decision would not be long. I rang again on 25 June and the lady checked the records. Yes, I had been granted public funding. The certificate was on its way. What? Are you sure? I wanted to cry and almost did. The lady sounded very happy for me. I told her that I had only expected a refusal, never a Yes. So, one door at last had not been banged in my face.

Things began happening fast from that point onwards. Adrian wrote to inform DEFRA that I had obtained public funding to return to court and asked them if they wished to continue. Again, he pointed out to them that I was simply not in a position to pay £13,000 to them. DEFRA wrote back on 23 July, offering to accept £4,000 and asked to see a copy of the funding certificate. They stated that they were 'extremely surprised that she has managed to obtain funding from the Legal Services Commission, and this is something which we reserve the right to take up with them directly.' Someone in DEFRA sounded outraged that I had actually obtained public funding against them, and indeed later on Legal Services tried but failed to claw back the funding they had granted me.

The Save Our Sheep Trust Fund now contained over £4,000 of funds, from donations sent in since February. Adrian told me that I had no choice left but to pay DEFRA, because even if I went back to court with public funding there was always the danger of more costs. Mr Flanagan said how surprised he was that Legal Services had granted the funding, and felt that this was the best deal on offer.

'You've driven DEFRA into the ground Janet,' he said one morning over the phone. 'I'd snatch their hand off for this offer if I was you.'

How I wish I had felt the same. I loathed going to the building society and asking for a cheque for DEFRA. I made sure that the cheque contained the name of the account; 'Save Our Sheep Appeal Fund'. We took the cheque to Adrian and shook hands as we left. He seemed almost as relieved as us that it was finally over. On 22 August DEFRA sent a letter, acknowledging the £4,000, in 'full and final settlement.' Adrian had informed them that the payment was made up of public donations, but they still cashed the cheque. So, after hounding me for six months, their 'pound of flesh' was other people's money.

53

Letting Go

So, at last it had all come to an end. The end was not ideal; not as I had wished, but nothing in life is ideal. I had done the best I could for the sheep, and had tried to keep my promise to them. Over 20,000 healthy sheep had been prematurely killed in the Brecon Beacons area by 16 August 2001, and how I wish the run up to the hearing had been swifter. However, with over 150,000 sheep grazing in the Brecon Beacons National Park, the loss could have been greater.

Somehow, I had feared that bailiffs would be a part of events, but I was still astonished that DEFRA resorted to such actions. Every aspect of the case, from beginning to end, was like a lesson; things had to be learned along the way, and sometimes there wasn't time to make the right decisions. The amazing help that we received from all kinds of people will stay with me forever.

If I had been a farmer, then a judicial review may have been more than a dream. After all, Peter Kindersley had been granted a review, back in March 2001. If only he had made the most of that opportunity. However, I have no regrets about taking the case forward. I believe that it had to be done, and someone had to make the move. DEFRA should not have been involved at all. The case should have been against the Welsh Assembly only, as it was clear from the evidence that Mr Jones, the Minister for Rural Affairs, was making the decisions.

All the evidence that gathered around the case pointed to wilful disregard of test results. As a lady at the Institute of Animal Health, Pirbright, told me over the phone:

'A negative test results means negative.'

Why would no official take heed of those results, which showed there was no disease in the many thousands of sheep consigned to death? The contiguous culling on the Brecon Beacons continued even when test results were known to be negative. What was the great rush to clear the Beacons of those wonderful creatures? There has been much conjecture, but no proper answer.

Premises where livestock was suspected of disease were declared Infected Premises before test results were even known, enabling rapid slaughter of all the healthy animals on contiguous farms. In Wales, according to official documentation, only 46 premises of the 117 listed Infected Premises returned positive test results for virus. In the county of Powys, only 33 out of 79 premises listed as Infected Premises had positive test results for virus (see table in Appendix 2, page 236).

Test results for the majority of contiguous farms in Wales were negative, as confirmed in the 'DEFRA Disease Control System Database as at 04/12/01,' which was placed in the House of Commons Library on 8 January 2002. In Powys only 5 out of 304 Dangerous Contact cases, (including contiguous premises), returned positive test results for FMD and they became listed as Infected Premises. At least 8 Dangerous Contact premises in Wales with negative test results became listed as Infected Premises, and remained so. The majority of test results for contiguous premises in England and Scotland were also negative.

Animals on contiguous premises were already being culled, as dangerous contacts, prior to the contiguous cull policy implemented on 27 March 2001 and of those premises tested, the vast majority of test results were returning as negative. Why then, was there any need to resort to a mathematical model that advocated slaughter on contiguous premises within 48 hours? The whole process was obscene and disgraceful, and furthermore, makes no sense whatsoever.

The statistics that relate to the infected premises, dangerous contacts, contiguous premises and slaughter on suspicion are horrifying. However, it must also be remembered that hundreds if not thousands of premises that lost their livestock are not even recorded. There were so many instances where animals were slaughtered under the livestock welfare disposal scheme, (LWDS), and there were also countless premises where animals were culled but which are not listed under any particular category.

If the courts had provided the opportunity for a judicial review, then the truth may have had the chance of tumbling out into the public domain. It was not to be though, and I have to accept that fact. The one great mercy is that no further mass cull of animals occurred throughout Wales after the judge ordered the hearing in August 2001. It was as if the light of the law, with all the possible consequences, proved a deterrent for any more killing.

In the absence of farmers' consent, the Ministers had no legal powers to slaughter animals in the 3km zone, or contiguously. This is why there was so much pressure placed on the farmers and graziers to sign the forms. In November 2003, the law changed. The Animal Health Bill became the amended Animal Health Act, giving the Ministers the very powers they had used illegally in 2001. Next time around there would be no requirement for the farmers to sign consent forms; their animals would be compulsorily slaughtered at the whims of the Ministers.

All that one can hope for is that a fairer system of government comes into being and that the very dangerous power to kill wherever a Minister decides will not be used.

Again, a judicial review of Government actions in 2001 would have made it very difficult for the Government to force through the Bill, as happened. The judiciary should give great consideration to the part it played in allowing the Government to walk away from their unlawful actions without any accountability.

The backbone of the Welsh countryside is farming. Take that away and the very fabric of our land will be destroyed. In Wales, as elsewhere in Britain, farmers are leaving the land at an alarming rate. To be unquestioning of government ethics and actions leaves open an extremely dangerous door, placing the future of our countryside in the hands of those who do not necessarily understand the way in which the country way of life has built up over centuries.

It is now February 2004 and the sheep are once again calling to their lambs in the fields behind our cottage. I love to hear those calls; there is a sort of safety in the sounds. For me, it means that our countryside is healing from the damage inflicted on it back in 2001. Damage not from any disease, but from Government policies out of control. The suffering of the sheep, cattle, goats and pigs in that year was horrific and must never be allowed to happen again. Their suffering was the reason for my attempt at obtaining justice. Justice was shelved for government expediency, but we have a right to ask for justice, and to keep asking. The thousands of healthy animals killed needlessly must not be forgotten.

There were times, during the case, when an overwhelming presence of sheep surrounded me. They would gather around as if spiritually willing me to keep fighting for them. Was this madness? Perhaps. The case had obsessed me and many people had told me to let go of it and get on with my life. I couldn't. The sheep haunted me; they had been so cruelly killed. Their voice had not been heard. I hope that this book gives them a voice. If it does, then I shall be content to let go.

Piping down the valleys wild
Piping songs of pleasant glee
On a cloud I saw a child.
And he laughing said to me.

Pipe a song about a Lamb;
So I piped with merry cheer,
Piper pipe that song again-
So I piped, he wept to hear.

Songs of Innocence (1789) introduction
William Blake 1757-1827

In memory of all the animals who were killed during the Foot and Mouth
Outbreak 2001.

Epilogue

A NEW POWER: THE ANIMAL HEALTH ACT 2002

On 6 November 2001, Elliot Morley, Parliamentary Under-Secretary of State for DEFRA, was giving evidence to the Environment, Food and Rural Affairs Select Committee. The subject being discussed was the Government's proposals for a new Animal Health Bill. The use of the word 'health' seems rather inappropriate, because the Bill sought to provide the ministers with unbridled powers of slaughter.

During the Foot and Mouth outbreak of 2001, the powers of slaughter vested in the Minister, or Ministers, as the case may be, had been provided by the Animal Health Act 1981. As I had found out to my cost, during the legal case taken against the mass culls, the Animal Health Act 1981 already gave the Minister extensive slaughter powers, and much seemed to depend on how these powers were interpreted. However, the phrases such as 'affected with foot-and-mouth disease or suspected of being so affected' and 'exposed to the infection of foot-and-mouth disease' contained within the 1981 Act provided a framework by which Ministers' powers could be constrained and questioned to a degree.

The new Bill was a much more dangerous piece of legislation. There was to be a new addition to the already wide slaughter powers contained within paragraph 3 of Schedule 3 of the 1981 Act. The new clause to be 'inserted' read:

'any animals the Secretary of State thinks should be slaughtered with a view to preventing the spread of foot-and-mouth disease.'

231

The following was also to be inserted:

'The Secretary of State may exercise the power under sub-paragraph (1)(c) whether or not animals:

(a) are affected with foot-and-mouth disease or suspected of being so affected;

(b) are or have been in contact with animals so affected;

(c) have been exposed to the infection of foot-and-mouth disease;

(d) have been treated with vaccine against foot-and-mouth disease.'

These new clauses effectively provided the Minister with unlimited slaughter powers, and in view of the Government's actions during 2001, these greater powers were immensely frightening. The new provisions paved the way for more mass culls in the future. Farmers and animal owners would no longer be in a position whereby they would be able to prevent their animals being culled. The Secretary of State was being given the power to kill wherever he/she chose; there was no longer any requirement to prove infection, suspicion of infection, or even exposure to disease.

As suspected by many individuals, these new powers were exactly the same as those used during 2001. Elliot Morley told the DEFRA Select Committee:

'At the present time, we do not have powers for a firebreak cull. There was the three-kilometre cull in Cumbria but that was a voluntary cull and people were invited to participate in that. Basically, if there were a situation where it was recommended that a firebreak cull would be desirable, then it gives you powers to do that.'

It was widely known that farmers had been under much pressure to comply with the demands for the firebreak culls not only in Cumbria, but also in Dumfries and Galloway and on the Brecon Beacons in Wales. In the absence of signed consent forms, no firebreak culls could lawfully have taken place. In theory the culls may have been voluntary, but in practice they were compulsory.

The Bill was met with much resistance from the House of Lords and on 26 March 2002, a brave move by Lord Moran caused it to be delayed until the autumn. However, on 7 November 2002 it finally became law, much to the dismay of many people.

Two law professors from Cardiff Law School, David Campbell and Robert Lee, had been researching the 2001 outbreak and in 2003 they published two legal papers: '*The Power to Panic: The Animal Health Act 2002*', and '*Carnage by Computer: The Blackboard Economics of the 2001 Foot and Mouth Epidemic*'.

Both papers are a fairly damning indictment of the Government's actions during 2001:

'The epidemic caused an economic loss which DEFRA estimates to be £9 billion. This figure is but a remote expression of the concrete losses, which include: the premature deaths of over 10 million animals, killed in ways which were almost always unacceptably, indeed criminally, inhumane and very often so horribly cruel as to be an occasion of lasting national shame; the loss of irreplaceable special breeds; the horror experienced by those with a scrap of humanity involved in the cull; the misery of thousands of small farmers and small business persons in areas related to farming and tourism whose incomes were drastically reduced, some of whom were driven into bankruptcy; the (continuing) pollution caused by disposal; the frustration of the enjoyment of the countryside for a year.'

Professors Campbell and Lee find that the, '2002 Act purports to legitimise a power to cull which need not stop at 10 million animals. It is difficult to see how, in a future epidemic, which did not stop when (or earlier than) the 2001 epidemic did, DEFRA will be able to avoid exceeding the 10 million figure, incurring and imposing even greater costs and, in particular, if stamping out without vaccination is used again, repeating the horrible cruelty.

'All sorts of revised contingency plans are being devised to make, *inter alia,* the stamping out of identified outbreaks of infection more effective. The executive clearly sees the general slaughter power it now enjoys as an important part of these plans. But it was a power exercised *ultra vires* as a response to the complete failure of contingency planning to identify infection, and it will only ever be used when this has happened again. Slaughter under reasonable suspicion was possible under the 1981 Act; the 2002 Act makes legal what a panic-stricken executive did in excess of the reasonable. There is, of course, no epidemiological practice that can guide a power to slaughter on this basis, for it is done, precisely, in the absence of reliable epidemiology; and so the executive will be no more able to exercise it sensibly now than it did when that exercise rightly was *ultra vires.' The Power to Panic.*

Of the contiguous cull policy, they state:

'This 'policy' emanated from a 10 Downing Street lobby briefing. The reader will hardly believe it, even in the context of this story, but no justification was then given or has ever since emerged for this central plank of what has passed for disease control policy (Anderson, 2002: para.10.3), and as the facts are now clearer and as a justification of impossible targets which occasion huge suffering is difficult, one imagines it never will.'

They also find that 'the contiguous cull certainly was a remote, abstract policy relying on bad information and wildly optimistic beliefs about slaughter disposal capacity which decayed into an unjustifiable massacre.' *Carnage by Computer.*

A Government that broke its own laws in 2001 should not have been allowed to change the law to their own advantage. Thus far, the Government has escaped true accountability, with weak promises of **'lessons to be learned'**. The horrific massacre of the animals in 2001 will happen again, as long as the power to kill remains. Next time it might be on such a scale as to make the nightmare of 2001 look merely like a bad dream.

Appendix 1

TEST RESULTS FOR HEFT AREAS ON BRECON BEACONS
(See MAP)

HEFT	RESULT	HEFT	RESULT
1a	1/825 antibody positive (VNT)	27	not tested
1b	10/738 antibody positive (VNT)	28	not tested
2	5/329 antibody positive (VNT)	29	negative
3	8/1065 antibody positive (VNT)	30	not tested
4	negative	31	not tested
5	68/815 antibody positive (VNT);	32	not tested
	re-test- 61/811 antibody positive	33	negative
5b	negative	34	negative
6	negative	35	not tested
7	negative	36	not tested
8	negative	37	not tested
9	negative	38	not tested
10	negative	39	negative
11	negative	40	negative
12	negative	41	negative
13	negative	42	not tested
14	negative	43	negative
15	negative	44	not tested
16	negative	45	not tested
17	negative	46	not tested
18	negative	47	not tested
19	negative	48	not tested
20	negative	49	negative
21	negative	50	negative
22	negative	51	negative
23	not tested	52	not tested
24	not tested	53	not tested
25	not tested	54	not tested
26	not tested	55	negative

Appendix 2

INFECTED PREMISES IN WALES – TEST RESULTS

COUNTY	IP Number	FMD +	antibody+	negative	untested	DATE
Gwynedd	13	+				27-Feb
Powys	19	+				28-Feb
Powys	22	+				28-Feb
Gwynedd	101	+				8-Mar
Powys	110			+		9-Mar
Gwynedd	122	+				9-Mar
Gwynedd	127			+		10-Mar
Powys	142	+				11-Mar
Powys	178				+	12-Mar
Powys	215	+				14-Mar
Powys	220			+		14-Mar
Powys	239			+		15-Mar
Gwynedd	242	+				15-Mar
Powys	251	+				15-Mar
Powys	255			+		15-Mar
Powys	259			+		16-Mar
Powys	262			+		16-Mar
Gwynedd	263				+	16-Mar
Gwent	272	+				16-Mar
Gwynedd	298	+				18-Mar
Gwynedd	311			+		18-Mar

COUNTY	IP Number	FMD +	antibody+	negative	untested	DATE
Gwynedd	314			+		19-Mar
Powys	345	+				19-Mar
Gwynedd	376			+		20-Mar
Gwynedd	384			+		20-Mar
Powys	395			+		20-Mar
Gwynedd	406	+				21-Mar
Gwent	429			+		21-Mar
Powys	433	+				21-Mar
Powys	461				+	22-Mar
Powys	465				+	22-Mar
Powys	469			+		22-Mar
Gwent	490				+	23-Mar
Powys	528			+		24-Mar
Powys	532				+	24-Mar
Powys	535				+	23-Mar
Gwynedd	573				+	25-Mar
Powys	588	+				25-Mar
Gwent	642				+	26-Mar
Powys	645			+		26-Mar
Powys	719	+				28-Mar
Gwent	733			+		31-Mar
Powys	753			+		29-Mar
Powys	794			+		30-Mar
Powys	836			+		30-Mar
Gwent	854	+				31-Mar
Gwent	867			+		31-Mar
Powys	869				+	1-Apr
Gwent	877			+		1-Apr
Gwent	899				+	2-Apr
Gwent	916			+		3-Apr
Powys	926	+				2-Apr
Powys	944	+				2-Apr
Gwent	946			+		3-Apr

COUNTY	IP Number	FMD +	antibody+	negative	untested	DATE
Powys	995			+		4-Apr
Powys	1055			+		5-Apr
Gwent	1058			+		6-Apr
Powys	1065			+		6-Apr
Gwent	1067			+		6-Apr
Gwent	1107			+		7-Apr
Gwent	1108			+		7-Apr
Powys	1156				+	9-Apr
Powys	1198				+	9-Apr
Powys	1205	+				10-Apr
Powys	1213			+		11-Apr
Powys	1233	+				11-Apr
Powys	1242	+				12-Apr
Powys	1247	+				12-Apr
Powys	1267			+		13-Apr
Powys	1281			+		13-Apr
Powys	1346	+				17-Apr
Powys	1385	+				18-Apr
Mid Glamorgan	1426				+	21-Apr
Powys	1456	+				24-Apr
Powys	1461	+				24-Apr
Mid Glamorgan	1470	+				25-Apr
Powys	1476			+		25-Apr
Powys	1479				+	25-Apr
Gwent	1490	+				27-Apr
Powys	1496			+		28-Apr
Gwent	1508			+		28-Apr
Gwent	1544			+		28-Apr
Gwent	1554			+		4-May
Powys	1565			+		8-May
Powys	1570	+				9-May
Powys	1580	+				11-May
Powys	1582			+		11-May

COUNTY	IP Number	FMD +	antibody+	negative	untested	DATE
Powys	1584	+				11-May
Powys	1596			+		14-May
Powys	1621			+		21-May
Gwent	1657	+				28-May
Powys	1779	+				23-Jun
Powys	1789		+			27-Jun
Powys	1796		+			29-Jun
Powys	1801		+ (1)			30-Jun
Powys	1806		+ (1)			2-Jul
Powys	1846	+				14-Jul
Powys	1848	+				14-Jul
Powys	1849	+				14-Jul
Powys	1852	+				15-Jul
Powys	1857	+				17-Jul
Powys	1860	+				18-Jul
Powys	1861	+				18-Jul
Powys	1868	+				18-Jul
Gwent	1869			+		19-Jul
Powys	1881				+	23-Jul
Gwent	1889	+				25-Jul
Powys	1891		+			26-Jul
Powys	1896	+				27-Jul
Powys	1897		+ (1)			27-Jul
Powys	1901		+ (1)			28-Jul
Powys	1907			+		30-Jul
Powys	1908			+		30-Jul
Gwent	1938	+				9-Aug
Powys	1939		+ (1)			9-Aug
Powys	1940			+		9-Aug
Powys	1945	+				12-Aug
TOTALS		46	8	47	16	

FURTHER READING

Fields of Fire, edited by Quita Allender (01934 844353)

Behind Chained Gates, Moira Linaker
£10, Hayloft Publishing, ISBN 1 904524 16 8

To Bid Them Farewell, A Foot and Mouth Diary, Adam Day
£14.50, Hayloft Publishing, ISBN 1 904524 10 6

The Impact of Foot and Mouth Disease: Environment, Food and Rural Affairs Committee, First Report of Session 2001-02
The Stationery Office, ISBN 0 215 00131 1

Plague, Pestilence and the Pursuit of Power, Steven Ransom
Credence Publications, ISBN 0 9535012 8 0

The Power to Panic: The Animal Health Act 2002, David Campbell and Robert Lee, Cardiff Law School and ESRC Research Centre for Business Relationships, Accountability, Sustainability and Society, (B.R.A.S.S.), UK.
Autumn issue of Public Law.

'Carnage by Computer': The Blackboard Economics of the 2001 Foot and Mouth Epidemic, David Campbell and Robert Lee, Cardiff Law School and B.R.A.S.S.
Social and Legal Studies 0964 6639, (200312) 12:4. SAGE Publications, London.

Report of the Committee of Inquiry on Foot-and-Mouth Disease 1968
HMSO, ISBN 10 14 2250 4